BIG BUSINESS
ITS GROWTH AND ITS PLACE

BIG BUSINESS

ITS GROWTH AND ITS PLACE

Prepared Under the Auspices of the
Corporation Survey Committee of the
Twentieth Century Fund, Inc.

ALFRED L. BERNHEIM
Editor

M. J. FIELDS
Assistant Editor

RUFUS S. TUCKER
Director of the Survey

MARGARET GRANT SCHNEIDER
Associate Research Director

NEW YORK
TWENTIETH CENTURY FUND, INC.
1937

FOREWORD

THIS VOLUME is the first of a series summarizing the results of a study of what is commonly known as "big business." The object of this first volume has been to put "big business" in its proper place against the whole background of American economic life.

Most studies in this field have been so exclusively focussed on the large companies themselves that the public has lost sight of those vast areas of American industry which are not incorporated at all, or in which the small or medium-size company predominates. This volume attempts to show how large big business bulks, in comparison with the smaller concern, on the American economic map as a whole and on the various sectors of the map which represent specific industries and groups of industries.

The larger study, of which this volume summarizes but a single part, was carried on by a special research staff of the Twentieth Century Fund, under the direction of Rufus S. Tucker. Its object was to find out, as far as the known facts can reveal them, the rôle of the giant corporation in American life. A Special Committee, under the chairmanship of Ralph E. Flanders, has had general charge of the undertaking. The Committee has been asked by the Trustees of the Fund to make a report, or a series of reports, to the public, on the problems which the research has disclosed, with constructive suggestions for their solution.

The Committee has decided, however, that before it makes its own report, summaries should be prepared and published of the most important parts of the factual material contained in the research reports. Alfred L. Bernheim was asked by the Fund to undertake this task. The present volume is the first fruit of his labors. In preparing this manuscript Mr. Bernheim and his assistants have also revised the original material in the light of data not available when the study was made.

As the reader will see, this book is purely factual. While certain conclusions are drawn from the facts they also are factual. Economic judgments and suggestions for action have been rigidly excluded. They are for the Special Committee to formulate, and at a later date.

Mr. Bernheim has been assisted by M. J. Fields, Assistant Editor, and Estelle Shrifte, and has had the benefit of the advice and counsel of Frederic Dewhurst, the Fund's Economist.

Dr. Tucker was assisted in preparing the original research findings by Margaret Grant Schneider, Associate Research Director of the study, and the following: C. D. Bremer, Clinton Collver, Edward P. Curl, L. V. Farra, M. J. Fields, Samuel E. Gill, Vladimir D. Kazakevich, Neil E. MacMillan, Betty Malakoff (Secretary), Carolyn H. Stetson, and William C. Willoughby.

EVANS CLARK, *Executive Director*
Twentieth Century Fund, Inc.

330 West 42nd Street
New York City
January 20, 1937

CONTENTS

TABLES

CHARTS

BIG BUSINESS
ITS GROWTH AND ITS PLACE

SUMMARY

1. The Growth and Extent of Incorporation

Corporations in America go back as far as the Colonial period. Up to 1800 at least 335 companies had been chartered, among which highway companies predominated. The first businesses to be incorporated were stage, turnpike, canal, water and insurance companies, and banking. In 1830 railroads began to appear, and by 1860 they occupied first place. It was not until after the Civil War, however, that the great expansion in the use of the corporate form in every branch of business activity got under way. It has continued in the twentieth century.

Partnerships and individual enterprises are, nevertheless, still very much on the business map. The widespread impression to the contrary is probably largely due to the fact that corporations are so conspicuous in certain branches of economic activity. In 1929 they accounted for about 86 per cent of the transportation and other public utility business, for about 92 per cent of manufacturing and for about 96 per cent of mining and quarrying. At the other extreme, however, stood agriculture, with corporations accounting for only about 6 per cent. For all branches of economic activity combined, including government, the corporate share in 1929 was only approximately 57 per cent. If government is excluded, the percentage rises to nearly 62.

2. THE RISE OF LARGE CORPORATIONS

The largest business enterprises of today—the "giants" with total assets of at least $50 million or total net income of at least $5 million each—are, however, almost exclusively corporations. The advantages of incorporation become more and more compelling as the size of a business enterprise grows and as the scope of its activities widens. Limited liability and facility for raising large amounts of capital are probably the two chief advantages of corporate organization.

Corporations become full-fledged giants either by internal growth—"plowing back" earnings into business or selling securities; or as the result of external growth—combining with other enterprises; or, more often, by both methods. The "combination movement" is responsible for a large proportion of America's industrial giants. It has assumed various more or less sharply differentiated forms at various more or less clearly distinguishable periods of time: "trusts," "holding companies," "consolidations," "mergers" and still other forms. The five years from 1898 through 1902 and the decade from the close of the World War to the collapse of the "New Era" boom, were the two periods in our history during which the combination movement was most prolific.

3. CONCENTRATION OF OPERATING UNITS

Industrial concentration can be measured by various standards. One is the frequency of "plural units"—combinations in which more than one industrial establishment is operated by a single central office. In 1929, according to the *Census,* only about one-eighth of the manufacturing enterprises were of the plural unit type, but this small fraction accounted for about 48 per cent of the wage-earners, 54 per cent of the value of the products and 50 per cent of the value added by manufacture of all manufacturing enterprises. Plural units were most frequent among corporate enterprises but were negligible among non-corporate.

Another measure is the size of the individual plant. In terms of number of wage-earners, the relative importance of the largest plant (more than 1,000) increased greatly between 1909 and 1919, until in the latter year nearly 27 per cent of all manufacturing wage-earners were employed in such plants. But between 1919 and 1929 this group lost ground slightly in relative position, to include a little more than 24 per cent of all wage-earners.

More significant as a measure of concentration than the size of the plant is the size of the entire enterprise. A special tabulation of the facts on the concentration of wage-earners in businesses in 84 manufacturing industries was made for the Twentieth Century Fund by the Bureau of the Census. More than one-half of the wage-earners in all manufacturing industries in 1933 were covered. The tabulation must not be considered as a representative cross-section, however, because the industries selected were mainly those in which a considerable degree of concentration was believed to exist.

Great differences were found between industries in the degree of concentration. At the one extreme was the cigarette industry in which about 99 per cent of the wage-earners were employed in the eight largest concerns and about 91 per cent in the four largest; at the other, was the women's clothing industry, in which less than 4 per cent of the wage-earners were employed in the six largest, and only approximately 2 per cent in the three largest enterprises. In 31 out of 82 industries more than two-thirds of all wage-earners were working for the 6 largest concerns. In 11 out of 80 industries, more than two-thirds of the wage-earners were employed by only 3 or 4 concerns. For 82 industries as a whole, the 512 largest concerns—1.6 per cent of the total number—employed approximately 37 per cent of all wage-earners. The 249 largest concerns in 80 industries—0.8 per cent of the total number—employed 27 per cent of all wage-earners.

The difference between the largest concerns and the rest of the industry was much narrower in the case of the distribution of establishments per concern than of the distribution of wage-earners per establishment.

The distribution of the value of products in each industry closely paralleled the distribution of the number of wage-earners. However the approximately 6 largest concerns showed a somewhat higher degree of concentration of value of products than of number of wage-earners in 40 out of 81 industries. For the approximately 3 largest concerns the degree of concentration of value of products was greater than that of number of wage-earners in 34 out of 79 industries, was less in 44 and was the same in 1.

Evidence of concentration is found in trade as well as in manufacturing. Nearly half of the wholesale business of the country was done by establishments of the plural unit type. In retail trade a fourth of the sales of 15 important kinds of business were made by chain stores in 1933. Four years earlier their share had been only a fifth.

4. CONCENTRATION OF CORPORATE WEALTH

Summaries of corporate income-tax returns published by the Bureau of Internal Revenue of the United States Treasury Department show that the 594 largest corporations in all fields, or 0.15 per cent of the total number,[1] owned approximately 53 per cent of total corporate assets in 1933. At the other extreme were 211,586 corporations with average total assets of less than $50,000 each. They comprised more than 54 per cent of the total number but owned only 1.4 per cent of the total corporate assets. Nearly 95 per cent of the total number of corporations had total assets averaging less than $1 million each, but this great bulk of corporate enterprises owned less than 15 per cent of total assets of all corporations.

Tremendous variations appear among the principal industrial divisions, which are concealed by overall averages. In transportation and other public utilities, 84 per cent of total assets were owned by the giant corporations which were only 1.2 per cent of all corporations in that field. In construction, on the other hand, only about 2.7 per cent (minimum estimate) of total assets were owned by the giant corporations which were only 0.01 per cent of the total number.

If the investments of corporations in other corporations are deducted from total assets in order to eliminate duplication, the share of the 594 largest corporations is slightly reduced—

---

1. Here, and throughout this volume, unless an exception is especially noted, such phrases as "total number" of corporations or "all" corporations should be understood to mean "all active reporting corporations submitting balance sheets."

from about 53 to about 50 per cent. Indeed, the share of all size classes of corporations having total assets of $1 million and over is lower. But if capital assets alone are considered (lands, buildings and equipment), the giant enterprises had control of 55 per cent of this form of assets in 1933. They owned 83 per cent of the physical plant in the transportation and other public utilities group, but only 11 per cent in the finance division.[2]

5. CONCENTRATION OF CORPORATE INCOME

The distribution of net income of all corporations reporting net income in 1933 also shows a high degree of concentration. Only 0.06 per cent of them—69 in number—had net incomes of $5 million and over, but in the aggregate they received about 30 per cent of the total net income of all income-reporting corporations. At the other end of the scale were nearly three-quarters of the profitable corporations, each with a net income of less than $5,000. Their combined share of total net income was less than 3 per cent. Not far from two-thirds of them had incomes of less than $1,000 each.

In 1933, 36 per cent of total net income went to the 0.2 per cent of profitable corporations that had assets of $50 million and over, and 79 per cent of the total net income went to the 6.2 per cent of corporations with total assets of $1 million and over. Income-reporting corporations with total assets of less

2. It should be observed that throughout Chapter 4 giant corporations are measured in terms of assets, and consequently when it is pointed out that giant corporations control a certain percentage of assets, corporations are being defined in those terms and none other. If size were measured by other standards, such as number of wage-earners, value added by manufacture or value of products, the relationship between the size classes might well be somewhat different.

than $1 million received less than 21 per cent of total net income though they accounted for nearly 94 per cent of the number of profitable corporations. The smallest total assets group —under $50,000—included nearly 47 per cent of all profitable corporations but received only 2.2 per cent of the total net income.

In transportation and other public utilities, about 68 per cent of the net income went to the giant corporations in 1933; in manufacturing, nearly 31 per cent; in trade, more than 25 per cent; in finance, nearly 18 per cent. The under-$50,000 class was of more importance in trade than in any other group, yet it received not quite 6 per cent of the total net income of this industrial division. Both in manufacturing and in transportation and other public utilities, less than 1 per cent of total net income went to the corporations in the smallest total assets class. In 1933 the giant corporations were, income-wise, of relatively less importance than they had been in either 1931 or 1932.

In each of the three years for which the comparison can be made, the corporations with total assets of $50 million and over showed a greater concentration of total assets than of net income. The discrepancy was greatest in 1933 when 200 great corporations owning about 56 per cent of the total assets of all corporations reporting net income, received only about 36 per cent of total statutory net income. The usual wide variations among industries occurred. In finance, for example, the concentration of assets was more than three times as great as the concentration of income; while in trade the concentration of income was actually greater by a small margin than the concentration of assets.

In 1933, 7,101 consolidated income-tax returns, representing groups of corporations closely connected by stock ownership, were filed. Of these 1,880 reported a net income, or 1.7 per cent of all corporations reporting a net income. But this 1.7 per cent accounted for nearly 28 per cent of the aggregate net income of all income-reporting corporations. This was a big decline from 1929, in which year corporations filing consolidated returns got about 51 per cent of the aggregate net income.

Within the consolidated group itself there was a very marked concentration of income. Of total net income reported on consolidated returns, 52 per cent went to corporations with incomes of $5 million and over. This compares with about 30 per cent for all profitable corporations, and with about 22 per cent for all profitable corporations other than those making consolidated returns. Concerns making consolidated returns were of varying importance in the different branches of industry. In transportation and other public utilities, 69 per cent of gross income (profitable and unprofitable corporations combined) was accounted for by consolidated returns in 1933. The corresponding figure for mining and quarrying was less than 14 per cent.

6. CONCENTRATION IN BANKING

During the present century the trend up to 1920 has shown a diffusion of banking resources, and thereafter a concentration. Bank failures and mergers were the factors most responsible for the increasing concentration in the latter period. The development of branch, group and chain banking also contributed.

As in the case of other groups of corporations, the few largest banks have a disproportionate economic importance. In 1934 national banks with capital stock of $5 million and over were only 0.7 per cent of all national banks in number, but they owned 47.2 per cent of all national bank assets and carried 47.8 per cent of all deposits in national banks. In 1925 the giant national banks were only 0.3 per cent of the total number of this class of banks, owned only 27.5 per cent of total national bank assets and carried only 27.7 per cent of national bank deposits. A study of the proportion of total loans and investments of all banks held by the country's twenty largest banking institutions shows that about 15 per cent was held by the twenty leaders in 1900 and about 27 per cent in 1931.

7. CONCENTRATION OF NATIONAL INCOME PRODUCED

In 1933 the 594 $50-million-and-over corporations accounted for 18.4 per cent of the total national income produced. If government is excluded, they accounted for 20.0 per cent. The "sub-giants" (4,229 with assets from $5 million up to $50 million) accounted for another 10.6 per cent (government included) or 11.6 per cent (government excluded). Less than 5,000 corporations accounted for 29.0 per cent of the estimated national income produced (government included), or for 31.6 per cent (government excluded).

Data for the giant corporations by separate branches of industry show the usual wide variations. Of the entire income produced by the transportation and other public utilities industry, 65.5 per cent was accounted for by corporations in the largest total assets class. Corresponding figures for the other branches are: manufacture, 33.4 per cent; finance, 17.0 per cent; trade, 7.4 per cent. In mining and quarrying, corporations with assets of $5 million and over (including twenty-one with assets of $50 million and over) produced nearly 61 per cent of the total income produced by all mining and quarrying enterprises, corporate and non-corporate.

8. CONCLUSIONS

No simple conclusions can be drawn. The large corporation is more or less important as the attention is focussed on special areas of American economic activity. Although only one-tenth of 1 per cent of the corporations in the country own more than half the nation's corporate assets, more than two-fifths of our entire economic activity is unincorporated. More than 81 per cent of it is carried on by partnerships and individuals, and by small and medium size corporations.

Specific industries and groups of industries vary strikingly in the degree of their concentration. No general rule can be laid down. Big business does not exist at all in agriculture or in clothing manufacture, at one extreme, while at the other it covers almost the entire field in public utilities and in some manufacturing industries, such as cigarettes, automobiles and steel.

It should be noted, however, that there are instruments of concentration and control—such as interlocking directorates, investment trusts, trade associations and banking affiliations—the influence of which does not, of course, appear in the statistics given in this volume.

Chapter 1

THE GROWTH AND EXTENT OF
INCORPORATION

THE CORPORATION as a form of business organization is not a new institution although its widespread use is relatively recent. Up to 1800 there had been 335 corporate charters issued in the United States, of which 295 had been obtained in the closing decade of the eighteenth century. Of the total number, 219 were for highway companies, 36 provided local public service, 67 were for banking and insurance and only 13 were classified under the head of "business (proper)."[1] The general types of corporations and dates of organization are given in Table 1.

Corporations Extend Their Sway

It is well known how the industrial revolution and the development of large scale production opened new opportunities for the employment of the corporate form of organization. Until the first quarter of the nineteenth century, however, corporations were created by special legislative acts. General incorporation laws were not enacted until 1829 in Massachu-

1. Business proper covers manufacturing, mining, agricultural, land and commercial enterprises.

TABLE 1

EIGHTEENTH CENTURY CORPORATIONS IN THE UNITED STATES,
BY GENERAL TYPES[a]

	Number of Charters by Types of Corporations				
Period	Financial	Highway	Local Public Service	Business (Proper)	Total
Colonial	1	..	5	1	7
1781–1785	5	5	..	1	11[c]
1786–1790	5	14	..	3	22[c]
1791–1795	29	78	4	3	114
1796–1800	27	122	27[b]	5	181[b]
Total	67	219	36[b]	13	335
Per cent	20.0	65.4	10.7	3.9	100.0

a. Derived from Joseph S. Davis, *Essays in the Earlier History of American Corporations,* II, 24.

b. Charters to water supply companies issued under the Massachusetts general incorporation Act of February 21, 1799 are not included.

c. The 33 charters granted in 1781–90 created but 25 distinct corporations.

setts, 1846 in Ohio and 1849 in New York.[2] Most of the states had general incorporation laws before the outbreak of the Civil War.

2. Adolf A. Berle, Jr., *Studies in the Law of Corporation Finance,* p. 20.

There seem, however, to have been isolated general incorporation acts, of little importance and slight effect, earlier than the dates mentioned by Berle. Davis, *op. cit.,* pp. 18–19, refers to a Massachusetts act of February 21, 1799, and states that "The act was probably utilized, for Massachusetts special acts incorporating water companies abruptly ceased in this year; but I have been unable to trace the companies so erected. It was not until 1811 that freedom of incorporation was extended to any important class of business corporations, and only in the forties did such acts become common in the United States." He also points out that "A North Carolina statute passed late in 1795, entitled 'an act to encourage the cutting of Canals by subscription' approximates a general incorporation act and has been called one. . . . The effect of this act is not clear. . . . It is doubted whether it proved of material importance, although a num-

Banks were among the first businesses to be incorporated in the United States. The earliest corporations included also stage, turnpike, canal, water and insurance companies. After 1830 railroads began to appear in increasing numbers, and by 1860 they occupied first place in the corporate lists.[3] About this time, too, gas companies began to be organized. In the post-Civil War period a tremendous expansion in the use of the corporate form of business organization occurred, and from that time on one area of economic life after another has come under its sway.

Chart 1 and Table 2 clearly indicate the growing importance of the corporation during the present century in the field of manufacture. The table also contains corresponding data for mining and quarrying.

Between 1904 and 1929 there was a steady increase in the degree of control exercised by corporations over American manufacturing enterprises. In 1904 corporations owned 23.6 per cent of the manufacturing establishments and produced 73.7 per cent of the value of products. Less than a generation later the percentage of establishments under the corporate form of organization had increased to 48.3, and these turned

ber of companies were probably organized under its authority." Berle, *op. cit.*, p. 20, refers to "The Act of Jan. 11, 1812, 10 Ohio Laws 24, was the first general incorporation act in Ohio. It authorized the formation of corporations for the purpose of manufacturing woolen, cotton, hemp or linen goods, etc. . . . This act, and corporations formed under it, was continued by the Act of Dec. 20, 1816, . . . but was repealed by the Act of Feb. 24, 1824 . . ." Charles W. Gerstenberg, *Materials of Corporation Finance*, pp. 31–33, states that the first general incorporation act in the United States including the grant of limited liability was the New York law of 1811.

3. Henry R. Seager and Charles A. Gulick, Jr., *Trust and Corporation Problems*, pp. 17–18.

CHART 1

GROWING IMPORTANCE OF THE CORPORATION IN
MANUFACTURING, 1904–1929

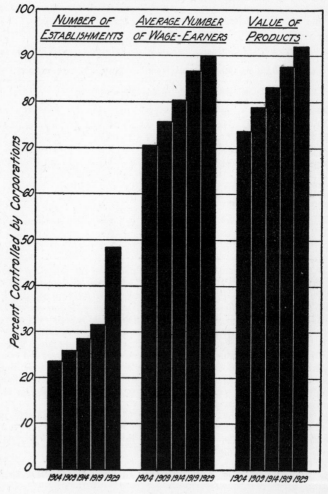

TABLE 2

CHANGING CHARACTER OF OWNERSHIP OF AMERICAN ENTERPRISES, 1904–1929

| | Percentage Distribution by Forms of Ownership | | | | | |
| | No. of Establishments | | Average No. of Wage-Earners | | Value of Products | |
Year	Corporations	Others	Corporations	Others	Corporations	Others
A. MANUFACTURING, 1904–1929[a]						
1904	23.6	76.4	70.6	29.4	73.7	26.3
1909	25.9	74.1	75.6	24.4	79.0	21.0
1914	28.3	71.7	80.3	19.7	83.2	16.8
1919	31.5	68.5	86.6	13.4	87.7	12.3
1929[b]	48.3	51.7	89.9	10.1	92.1	7.9
B. MINING AND QUARRYING, 1902–1929[c]						
1902	28.6[d]	71.4	85.0	15.0	86.3	13.7
1909	35.4[d]	64.6	90.6	9.4	91.4	8.6
1919	51.1[e]	48.9	94.2	5.8	93.6	6.4
1929	63.0[e]	37.0	94.7	5.3	95.7	4.3

a. Percentages computed from data obtained from the following sources: For 1904, 1909, 1914, 1919, United States Department of Commerce, Bureau of the Census, *Abstract of the Census of Manufactures, 1919*, p. 340; for 1929, same source, *Fifteenth Census of the United States: 1930, Manufactures: 1929*, I, 95. In order to save space, further reference to *Census* material will give only the title of the publication and will not repeat the name of the source.

b. The 1929 *Census* figures omit establishments producing goods valued at less than $5,000 per annum. In the case of wage-earners employed and value of products this omission does not influence the percentages significantly. But the number of establishments is materially reduced through the exclusion of small, mostly unincorporated, plants and that gives a decided upward bias to the percentage of corporate ownership.

c. *Mines and Quarries*, 1902, V, 68; 1909, XI, 33; 1919, XI, 29; 1929, p. 14. 1929 percentages computed. Figures in the *Census of Mines and Quarries* are not strictly comparable from year to year because of different classifications in the mining industries in the various years.

d. Percentage of number of operators.

e. Percentage of number of enterprises. An enterprise may include more than one pit.

out more than 92 per cent of the value of products. About 90 per cent of all manufacturing wage-earners were in 1929 employed by corporations as compared with 71 per cent a quarter of a century earlier.

Developments in mining and quarrying have been similar to those in manufacturing.

Incorporation by Branches of Economic Activity, 1929

Because corporations are so conspicuous in many branches of economic activity; and because there is a widespread interest in corporate securities and an almost continuous political and legislative concern over the affairs of large corporations, there is a popular impression that individual and partnership enterprises have vanished with the horse and buggy. This impression is more or less correct—but only more or less—as to the transportation and other public utilities industry, as to manufacturing as a whole and as to mining and quarrying. But it is not at all correct as far as the other branches of economic activity are concerned. These other branches, including government,[4] produced 63.3 per cent of the national income in 1929[5] as against only 36.7 per cent produced by the above named groups. Of total economic activity, in terms of income produced, only 57 per cent was conducted through incorporated profit-seeking businesses. Table 3 and Chart 2 give the data for each of ten principal branches of economic activity.

4. Government must, of course, be considered as an income-producing industry by virtue of the fact that it renders services of many kinds to the community (and to some extent produces commodities), in exchange for taxes paid as the price for these services.

5. Later figures are available but it is believed that, for the purposes at hand, they are not as pertinent as those for 1929.

TABLE 3

RELATIVE IMPORTANCE OF VARIOUS BRANCHES OF ECONOMIC
ACTIVITY, AND PER CENT OF TOTAL INCOME PRODUCED
BY CORPORATIONS IN EACH BRANCH, 1929

	Per Cent of National Income Produced[a]	Per Cent of Income Produced by Corporations in Each Branch (Estimated)[b]
Government[c]	7.8	..[d]
Agriculture and related industries	9.1	6
Construction	3.7	33
Miscellaneous	5.2[e]	33
Service: professional, amusements, hotels, etc.	10.2	33
Finance: banking, insurance, real estate, holding companies, stock and bond brokers, etc.	13.6[e]	56
Trade	13.7	63
Transportation and other public utilities	11.1	86
Manufacturing	23.3	92
Mining and quarrying	2.3	96
All branches	100.0	57

a. United States Senate, 73 Cong. 2 Sess., *Doc. 124,* "National Income, 1929–32." Above percentages computed from original data after a few changes in classifications were made. See footnote e.

b. Sufficient space is not available to explain the methods used to arrive at the estimates of the percentage of income produced by corporations. The underlying data came from various sources, primarily: *Doc. 124,* cited in the preceding footnote; United States Treasury, Bureau of Internal Revenue, *Statistics of Income for 1929; Fifteenth Census of the United States: 1930, Construction Industry; Distribution,* I, *Retail Distribution,* Part I; *Distribution,* II, *Wholesale Distribution; Manufactures: 1929,* I; *Mines and Quarries: 1929.*

c. See p. 16, footnote 4.

d. Government corporations, such as the Reconstruction Finance Corporation, the Home Owners' Loan Corporation, the Federal Deposit Insurance Corporation, as well as towns and other forms under which many local government units are incorporated, are not subject to taxation and involve no question of

CHART 2
RELATIVE IMPORTANCE OF VARIOUS BRANCHES OF ECONOMIC
ACTIVITY, 1929, AND RELATIVE IMPORTANCE OF
CORPORATIONS IN EACH BRANCH, 1933

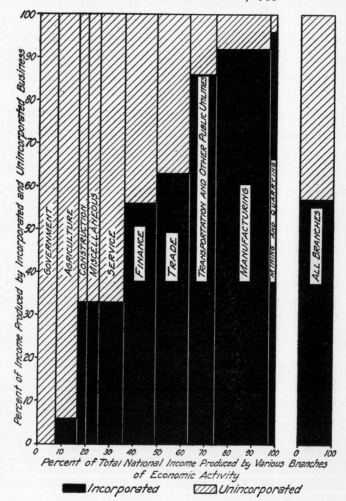

The wide variation in the extent to which the major branches of economic activity are organized under the corporate form of ownership is striking. With the exception of government, which from the point of view of this volume presents no corporation problem, agriculture leaves the largest area to individual owners and partnerships. From only 6 per cent in agriculture, the domination of the corporation ranges up to 92 and 96 per cent, or almost complete control, in manufacturing and mining, respectively.

As a breakdown is made of each major group into its component parts, internal variations appear that are even wider than among the groups themselves. For example, domestic service, conducted largely as individually-owned enterprises, and motion picture production, almost entirely incorporated, are in *Statistics of Income* both included under "service," which embraces professional service, amusements, hotels, etc. But as a group, service is 33 per cent incorporated.

Other Measures of Extent of Incorporation

Estimating the extent of incorporation in terms of national

domination of a branch of industry by individuals or groups motivated by a desire for profits. They are not here regarded, therefore, as "incorporated business." Similarly, universities, hospitals, and other non-profit seeking institutions are not here regarded as "incorporated business" and are, therefore, included among the unincorporated enterprises.

e. In order to facilitate comparisons with figures from *Statistics of Income,* estimated income produced by the brokerage branch of business has been subtracted from the figures of the "miscellaneous" group, in which brokerage was included in "National Income, 1929–32," and added to the "finance, banking, etc." group in which brokerage is included in the Bureau of Internal Revenue figures. This change gives to finance and banking 13.6 per cent instead of 11.6 per cent and to miscellaneous industries 5.2 per cent instead of 7.2 per cent of national income produced.

income is one method of measurement. It is well to realize, however, that it is not the only one, and also that other methods give different results. Consider, for instance, manufacturing and mining and quarrying. In the former, 92 per cent of the value of products was, in 1929, under the control of corporations, but somewhat less than 90 per cent of the wage-earners were employed by corporations and only about 48 per cent of the number of establishments were corporate owned.[6] Corresponding figures for mining and quarrying are 96, 95 and 63 per cent, respectively.[7]

6. *Fifteenth Census of the United States: 1930, Manufactures: 1929*, I, 95.
7. *Fifteenth Census of the United States: 1930, Mines and Quarries: 1929*, p. 14.

Chapter 2

THE RISE OF LARGE CORPORATIONS

"BIG BUSINESS" in the United States manifests itself today almost exclusively in the corporate form—and has done so for many years. Some kinds of financial companies are the principal exceptions. The two chief advantages of incorporation are limited liability and a high effectiveness in raising capital. These advantages apply with increasing force as the property that is owned increases in value and scope. They probably account for the almost universal use of the corporate form on the part of our large enterprises.

Large Corporations Defined

Largeness is a term which takes on meaning only in relation to a standard and every standard must be more or less arbitrarily determined. The study on which this volume is based has selected for its standard of financial largeness any corporate enterprise which controls at least $50 million of assets, or earns a net income of at least $5 million per year, because these figures represent the largest size groups in the annual tabulations of income made by the Bureau of Internal Revenue of the United States Treasury Department.

Obviously, this "dead level" standard cannot be applied to

periods far apart in time or differing widely in their economic characteristics. The early New England textile mills, which were huge for their time and which loomed so large in the eyes of their competitors, would be negligible by these standards today. So too is the dead level standard likely to distort comparisons between industries at any given time. An enterprise may be much smaller than the bottom limits of largeness set forth above, and yet it may be large and correspondingly influential and powerful in its particular industry. In another industry, an enterprise which qualifies statistically as large may be relatively small and unimportant.[1]

But standards that shift for time and location and industry present difficulties of their own. For example, with different standards of largeness for different industries, a $50 million corporation and a $1 million one might both come under the head of large, which for some purposes would be illogical. To those who collected and analyzed the data used in this pamphlet, the dead level standard, though not perfect, seemed better adapted to the objects of their study than the shifting standard.

Internal versus External Growth

Large corporations have come into being in various ways: as a result of growth nourished by earnings "plowed back" into the enterprise; through the sale of securities to the public to finance expansion; and as a result of mergers, or combina-

1. It is worth noting, too, that an enterprise may be very large in the aggregate, but if it functions in a number of more or less sharply differentiated industries—as many large enterprises do—it may play a minor rôle compared to its specialized competitors in some of the separate industries.

tions of some other type such as trusts and holding companies. Growth resulting from plowing back earnings or from the expansion of the original unit may be thought of as internal growth; the other as external growth.

Internal growth for an expanding economy as a whole, except for occasional interruptions during depressions, is a continuous process. It is merely one manifestation of the accumulation of savings on the part of the community. External growth, on the other hand, apparently occurs in more or less sharply defined waves, and it takes various forms which will be briefly discussed.

Three General Types of Combinations

Combinations may be broadly classified into three general types: the horizontal, the vertical and the newer, complementary type.

A horizontal combination is a combination of concerns previously engaged in producing similar goods, or goods that can be substituted for each other. More than either of the other types, its immediate purpose is to reduce competition.

A vertical combination involves the union of companies producing certain materials with other companies which utilize these materials; or else a combination of producing companies with companies selling their products. Vertical combinations do not necessarily limit competition. Indeed they sometimes make competition so intense as to induce the formation of horizontal combinations.

A complementary combination involves the union of concerns producing goods of a different nature from each other, but which are constantly used together by consumers. This type of consolidation is sometimes called "circular." Like the vertical, it is not necessarily inconsistent with the maintenance of vigorous competition.

Trusts

Trusts are one manifestation of industrial combinations. The earliest form of trust activity, and one that is still common, is the "gentlemen's agreement." A somewhat more complicated type is the "pool," which, in a broad sense, is a set of agreements whereby separate business entities seek to harmonize their policies for their mutual benefit. Although pools still persist they were in vogue mainly in the two decades following the Civil War. The classification of types or their sequence is a more or less arbitrary procedure; but next in order might be listed the trust proper.[2] Technically, the trust was a device by which legally independent corporations were managed by a joint board of trustees. The first trust of national significance was the Standard Oil Company, organized in 1879.[3]

Regardless of the form it uses, the trust or combination movement represents a tendency toward the unification of interests for such purposes as reducing competition, effecting economies and acquiring wider control over markets—with increased profits, of course, the ultimate goal. In respect to all of these, the trust proper was far more effective than either

2. Trade associations or interlocking directorates, in so far as they figure in the trust movement at all, may be thought of chiefly as a means of effecting gentlemen's agreements of some sort or other.

3. William Z. Ripley, editor, *Trusts, Pools and Corporations.*

the gentlemen's agreement or the pool because the successful operation of these depended largely on good faith rather than on the existence of a contractual obligation, which was the essence of the trust. Trusts, in this sense, were almost entirely abolished by decisions of state courts in the early nineties on the ground that they were inconsistent with the charters of the corporations composing them,[4] or else, since they tended to monopoly, that they were contrary to public policy and void.[5] Today the word "trust" is loosely applied to any large corporation which has, or is popularly believed to have, some degree of monopolistic control in its industry, as, for instance, the "Steel Trust" or the "Aluminum Trust."

Holding Companies and Mergers

An effective substitute for the trust is the holding company. Indeed, the holding company was so obviously a device for accomplishing what the courts condemned in the trust form of organization that there was some question as to its legality from the very beginning. This, no doubt, partly explains why, although the State of New Jersey had opportunely amended its corporation law to legalize the holding company in 1889, the device did not begin to become common until the opening of the present century. The chief reason, however, was the dullness in business and the lack of confidence among investors which followed the panic of 1893–1894. Although holding companies were not unknown before 1889, corporations had usually not been allowed to hold stocks of other corpora-

4. *People v. The North River Sugar Refining Co.,* 121 N.Y. 582 (1890).
5. *State v. Standard Oil Co.,* 49 Ohio State 137 (1892).

tions until then.

Ordinarily, holding companies are not organized to engage in actual operations, but rather to acquire control, through stock ownership, over operating companies—either new ones or concerns already successfully established. Purely investment concerns, such as investment trusts, which make no attempt to exercise control over the activities of the corporations in which they hold stock, are generally not considered holding companies. Holding companies are organized to coordinate the activities of their affiliates, to assist them in financing and to provide them with various kinds of technical services, such as engineering, accounting and advertising.

The holding company as a device for combining business concerns was intended to provide an escape from anti-trust legislation, and has, on the whole, been relatively free from attack under the anti-trust laws. This is not to say that laws have not been passed to prevent its employment where its effect is to create a monopoly. Quite the contrary, the Northern Securities decision cited the provisions of the Sherman Act in disapproving the device in railroading. Section 7 of the Clayton Act specifically states that it is illegal for a corporation engaged in interstate commerce to acquire the stock of another corporation so engaged where the acquisition might result in a substantial lessening of competition between the two companies.

The Transportation Act of 1920 undertook to give to the Interstate Commerce Commission power to prevent the control of one railway company by another such company through stock ownership,[6] but the Commission itself has held that it

6. Par. 2, sec. 5.

could not thereby prevent the control of an operating railway concern by a pure holding company. This decision has the support of a lower court.[7] Among the most important provisions of the Banking Act of 1933 was one to divorce member banks from their security company and holding company affiliates.[8] More recently, the Public Utility Act of 1935 has subjected public utility holding companies to rigid federal supervision; and, under some circumstances, it seeks to abolish them.

Growth of Combinations to 1905

Combinations reported in the *Census* amounted to only 5 between 1861 and 1885, but ranged from 4 to 79 in each year thereafter—199 in all—until and including 1900.[9] The peak year was 1899. Some of the most important combinations, however, were excluded from this count because of the narrow definition employed by the *Census*.

The organization of trusts before 1897 can hardly be said to have attained the dignity of a movement. But, beginning in that year, a phenomenal prosperity set in and created a powerful stimulus. In 1897 there were about 44 corporations, or allied groups of corporations, with $50 million or more capital. Only eight of them, however, were industrials and eleven or twelve public utilities. The majority were railroads. By the end of 1900, the number of fifty-million-dollar industrial corporations had risen to 29; by the end of 1903, to 41. According to Moody, there were 305 "trusts," with an aggregate

7. *Forty-third Annual Report of the Interstate Commerce Commission*, 1929, pp. 80–82. In re: *Stock of Denver & Rio Grande Western R. R.*, 70 I.C.C. 102.
8. The Banking Act of 1935 made no substantial alteration in this provision.
9. *Twelfth Census of the United States: 1900*, VII, *Manufactures*, part I, pp. lxxv–lxci.

capitalization in excess of $6.5 billion, in actual operation at the beginning of 1904. In addition, 13 more, with an aggregate capitalization exceeding $500 million, were in process of reorganization or readjustment. Of these 318, 82, with a total capitalization of nearly $1.2 billion, were organized before 1898, and 236, with a total capitalization of more than $6 billion, came into being between the beginning of that year and January 1, 1904.[10]

Professor Watkins reported data concerning industrial consolidations between 1890 and 1904.[11] These are given in Table 4. Of the fifteen years covered, the five from 1898 through 1902 accounted for more than 70 per cent of the total number of consolidations and for more than 81 per cent of the total capitalization of the consolidated companies. Throughout this early period, a considerable portion of the total capitalization of the combined concerns was "water."

10. John Moody, *The Truth About the Trusts,* pp. 453–469, 486. Moody uses the word "trust" to embrace "every act, agreement, or combination of persons or capital believed to be done, made, or formed with the intent, power, or tendency to monopolize business, to restrain or interfere with competitive trade, or to fix, influence, or increase the prices of commodities."

11. Myron W. Watkins, *Industrial Combinations and Public Policy,* Appendix II, pp. 317–324. In gathering his material, Professor Watkins observed the following criteria:

"First, purely local combinations have been omitted. . . . Second, public utility mergers have not been included. Third, a combination of American properties under a foreign charter and effected by foreign interests has been included. . . . Fourth, duplications on account of expansion, or reorganization accompanied by more comprehensive combination, in successive years, have been allowed, but not when the combination and the recombination were effected in the same year. Piecemeal expansion, even by the merger process, has of necessity been excluded from consideration. Fifth, consolidations with a capitalization of less than one million dollars have been excluded. . . ." *Ibid.,* p. 39.

TABLE 4

INDUSTRIAL CONSOLIDATIONS, 1890–1904

Date	Number of Consolidations	Capitalization
1890	11	$ 137,611,500
1891	13	133,597,167
1892	12	170,017,000
1893	5	156,500,000
1894	..	....
1895	3	26,500,000
1896	3	14,500,000
1897	6	75,000,000
1898	18	475,250,000
1899	78	1,886,050,000
1900	23	294,500,000
1901	23	1,632,310,000
1902	26	588,850,000
1903	8	137,000,000
1904	8	236,194,000
Total	237	$5,963,879,667

After 1904 the combination movement practically stopped, not to be resumed until after the World War. In that interval many corporations grew in size, and some of the existing combinations were reorganized to conform to the decisions of the Supreme Court.[12] Although there were sporadic mergers, no general outburst comparable to that ending in 1904 occurred. In some of the newer industries, however, such as aluminum,

12. Especially in accordance with the views of the Court in *Northern Securities Company v. United States,* 193 U.S. 197 (1904) ; and in *The Standard Oil Company of New Jersey v. United States,* 221 U.S. 1 (1911).

motor vehicles and motion pictures, some large organizations did come into existence—not so much by combination as by internal growth.

Reasons for Suspension of Combination Movement

Various explanations have been offered for the virtually complete suspension of the combination movement for more than fifteen years, all of which appear to have some validity. One of these is the "trust-busting" activities of the Roosevelt and Taft administrations. Another is the unprofitableness of a large number of combinations formed before 1905, of which very few lived up to the expectations of their promoters. Still another plausible explanation is based on the fact that the successful promotion of trusts, holding companies, mergers and business combinations of every nature depends largely upon the existence of an optimistic, not to say a credulous, body of investors and speculators liberally supplied with funds— either their own or borrowed from banks. The stock market crash of 1903 and the business crisis of 1907, however, taught both individual purchasers and banks a severe lesson from which they did not recover for several years. The 1929 stock market collapse and subsequent business depression had the same effect and brought an abrupt close to the combination movement of the "New Era" of the twenties.

Combinations in Post-War Decade

It was not until after the World War that conditions were ripe for a revival of the combination movement on a large scale, although the war profits of the preceding years had unexpectedly made possible the rejuvenation of some of the older organizations that had been failures.

TABLE 5
NUMBER OF MERGERS RECORDED IN MANUFACTURING AND MINING, BY INDUSTRIES, 1919–1928[a]

	1919	1920	1921	1922	1923	1924	1925	1926	1927	1928	Total
Oil	15	35	16	11	9	9	8	7	7	7	124
Coal	4	7	6	5	8	11	5	5	3	4	58
Iron and steel	24	42	9	15	13	27	25	23	57	35	270
Nonferrous	6	6	12	6	5	6	15	25	22	19	121
Textiles	4	8	8	6	6	9	7	11	9	36	104
Motor vehicles	8	12	7	5	5	4	9	6	5	6	67
Chemicals	1	5	4	3	3	6	2	8	8	19	59
Foodstuffs	8	16	9	5	8	7	13	14	25	23	128
Lumber and paper	3	10	8	4	1	2	6	12	25	20	91
Other	16	32	10	8	9	14	31	28	46	52	246
Total	89	173	89	67	67	95	121	139	207	221	1,268

a. Willard L. Thorp, "The Changing Structure of Industry," *Recent Economic Changes in the United States*, I, 186. Thorp points out that "... no pretense is made that the record here given is complete." However, he expresses his belief that we can, nevertheless "... assume, with some justification, that the records will indicate the trend if not the absolute amount of the movement." *Ibid.*, pp. 182–183.

For the post-War period Dr. Thorp has compiled a record of combinations in manufacturing and mining, part of which is reproduced in Table 5.

During the ten years, 1919–1928, there were 1,268 combinations in manufacturing and mining, of which one-third took place during the boom years, 1927 and 1928. The movement seems to have been particularly active in the iron and steel industry, although more than 100 combinations occurred also in each of the oil, nonferrous metals, textiles and foodstuffs industries. The 1,268 combinations involved the union of 4,135 separate concerns and the disappearance of 5,991.[13]

Thorp has also compiled some figures[14] on consolidations among public utilities, based on data published in the *Electrical World.* These show that from 1919 through 1927 a total of 3,744 public utility companies disappeared, either through their merging or being acquired by other companies. The trend of the number of disappearing companies was steadily upward, with two interruptions, from 22 in 1919 to 1,029 in 1926. There was a drop to 911 in 1927.[15]

The post-War combinations were marked by two tendencies: the growth of holding companies, as distinguished from larger operating companies, especially in the field of public utilities; and the rise of marketing rather than production problems as determinants of the nature of combinations. The

13. In 1929, 1,245 independent manufacturing and mining enterprises disappeared, and in 1930, 747. Thorp, "The Persistence of the Merger Movement," *The American Economic Review, Supplement,* March 1931, pp. 76–89.
14. *Recent Economic Changes in the United States,* I, 185, 187.
15. In the first three quarters of 1928 there were 90 fewer disappearances than in the corresponding period in 1927.

latter resulted in the creation of complementary, sometimes called circular, combinations; and also in the rapid growth of chain stores.

Generally speaking, the post-War manufacturing and mining combinations involved less capital and resulted in the formation of smaller units than did those before the War— but there were many more of them. They included not only complementary combinations but also the older horizontal and vertical types. In addition, many concerns during the decade of the twenties grew, without combining, to such size that they were considered by some observers to occupy a semi-monopolistic position.

The emphasis in this chapter has been on growth through combinations, but the fact should not be lost sight of that the reinvestment of profits by businesses is also an important cause of corporate growth, especially during certain periods of time and in certain industries. The same may be said of internal expansion through funds obtained from the sale of securities to the public.

Chapter 3

CONCENTRATION OF OPERATING UNITS

A. MANUFACTURING

THE FIRST official survey of concentration in manufacturing was undertaken by the United States Bureau of the Census in 1900. It listed 185 combinations embracing 2,040 separate active establishments, which accounted for 8.4 per cent of the wage-earners, 9.6 per cent of the wages and 14.1 per cent of the value of products of all establishments. The remainder in each instance was accounted for by 294,400 establishments.[1] To put it another way, although the 185 industrial combinations comprised less than 1 per cent of all establishments, they controlled more than 8, 9 and 14 per cent of the laborers, wages and value of manufactured products, respectively. As measured by the share of the total value of products, the highest degrees of concentration were found in the following fields: chemicals, 33.4 per cent; iron and steel, 28.4 per cent; tobacco, 26.2 per cent; metals and metal products other than iron and steel, 24.1 per cent. The number of combinations in the chemicals industry was 15 (250 plants); in iron and steel, 40 (447

1. All establishments consist of the 296,440 "all other establishments" classified by the *Census*. They do not include 215,814 hand trades, 127,419 establishments with a product of less than $500, 138 governmental establishments and 383 educational, eleemosynary and penal institutions.

34

plants) ; in tobacco, 4 (41 plants) ; in metals and metal products, 11 (89 plants).[2]

Plural Units and Single Units Contrasted

On the general subject of concentration, figures are available of a different character from those in the *Census* of 1900. For example, Willard L. Thorp has made a study of ". . . combinations in their simplest and most openly acknowledged form—combinations in which more than one industrial establishment is operated by a single central office. . . ."[3] For convenience one may call these "plural unit enterprises" as distinguished from "single unit enterprises" though Thorp himself does not employ these terms. In 1919, there were, according to Thorp, 21,464 manufacturing establishments embraced by plural unit enterprises, and these comprised 7.4 per cent of all manufacturing enterprises.[4] This figure included all plural unit enterprises no matter how they had developed, whether by some form of merger or consolidation, or by internal growth or by purchase.

In 1929 the number of plural unit establishments recorded by the *Census* was 26,286, or 12.5 per cent of the total.[5] These figures are not comparable with Thorp's, since in 1929 the *Census* omitted establishments producing less than $5,000 per annum. Had they been included, the percentage of plural unit

2. *Twelfth Census of the United States, op. cit.,* pp. lxxx–lxxxi.
3. Willard L. Thorp, "The Integration of Industrial Operation," *Census Monographs—III,* p. 17. Thorp goes on to say: ". . . Financial combination, interlocking directorates, bank control—all such obscure forms of relationship are disregarded. This is a study of *operating* combinations. . . ."
4. *Ibid.,* p. 107.
5. *Fifteenth Census of the United States, Manufactures: 1929,* I, 95.

establishments would undoubtedly have been smaller than 12.5, but probably would still have been larger than in 1919, showing an increase in concentration during the decade—to the extent that plural units are a criterion of concentration.

The following table, based on the 1929 *Census,* shows the relative importance, in accordance with various standards, of plural and single units. The data are subdivided between corporate owned and non-corporate owned enterprises.

TABLE 6

PERCENTAGE DISTRIBUTION OF PLURAL AND SINGLE UNIT
MANUFACTURING ENTERPRISES, 1929[a]

	Corporate		Non-Corporate		Total	
	Plural Units	Single Units	Plural Units	Single Units	Plural Units	Single Units
Number of establishments	11.6	36.7	0.8	50.9	12.4	87.6
Number of wage-earners	47.6	42.3	0.8	9.3	48.4	51.6
Value of products	53.7	38.5	0.6	7.2	54.3	45.7
Value added by manufacture	48.9	42.6	0.6	7.9	49.5	50.5

a. *Ibid.* Percentages computed from data in the *Census.*

When we look at the total column, we see that, in terms of number of establishments, manufacturing enterprises were in 1929 still predominantly of the single unit type. But in other respects—number of wage-earners, value of products and value added by manufacture—the distribution between the single and plural unit types was nearly even.

When corporate and non-corporate enterprises are considered separately, it becomes evident that virtually all unincorporated business was of the single unit type. Even among corporations there were still more than three times as many single as plural unit enterprises; but in respect to the number of wage-earners, value of products and value added, the plural unit concerns bulked larger than the single unit.

Presence of Large Plants in Manufacturing Industries

The extent of the existence of plural units is one measure of concentration in manufacturing industries. Another is the size of the unit, or plant. Various yardsticks can be used to determine whether a plant is large or small and to compare plants with each other as to their relative size—the number of wage-earners employed, the value added by manufacture, the horse power used, for example. Everything considered, the number of wage-earners employed seems the most feasible and appropriate unit of measurement. But this measure is by no means free from shortcomings because over a period of time conditions of employment and productive processes change. More than 1,000 employees seems a reasonable, though arbitrary, definition of largeness as applied to a manufacturing plant.[6]

Table 7 shows the percentage distribution of wage-earners among plants in all manufacturing industries for various census years through 1929.

6. The use of a "dead level" standard has been discussed on pp. 21–22. The selection of 1,001 as the bottom limit of largeness cannot, of course, be defended against any other number within a reasonable distance of it, plus or minus, but, on the other hand, neither does any other number seem more appropriate than 1,001.

TABLE 7

PERCENTAGE DISTRIBUTION OF THE NUMBER OF WAGE-EARNERS
PER PLANT, ALL MANUFACTURING INDUSTRIES, 1909–1929[a]

Number of Wage-Earners Per Plant	Percentage Distribution of Wage-Earners in Plants Classified According to Number of Wage-Earners					
	1909	1914	1919[b]	1921	1923	1929
1 to 5	4.7	4.5	(2.7) 3.4	3.2	2.4	3.2
6 to 20	9.7	8.6	(6.8) 6.9	8.6	7.0	6.7
21 to 50	11.6	10.5	9.1	11.2	9.3	9.2
51 to 100	11.8	11.3	9.8	11.3	10.1	10.1
101 to 250	19.0	18.8	(17.6) 17.4	19.1	17.9	18.0
251 to 500	15.2	15.3	(13.9) 13.8	14.6	15.2	15.1
501 to 1,000	12.7	13.2	(13.4) 13.2	12.3	14.0	13.3
1,001 and over	15.3	17.8	(26.7) 26.4	19.7	24.1	24.4
Total	100.0	100.0	100.0	100.0	100.0	100.0

a. The percentages have been computed from data published in the censuses of manufactures for various years.

b. The censuses of 1909, 1914 and 1919 included establishments with value of products less than $5,000. Subsequent censuses excluded these small establishments. But the 1929 *Census of Manufactures* gave figures for 1919 corrected by the elimination of the under-$5,000 establishments. These corrected figures appear in parentheses in Table 7. They are comparable with those in the later censuses. Those for 1909 and 1914, strictly speaking, are not. But as can be seen from the 1919 figures, the corrections have very little effect upon the percentage distribution of wage-earners.

Large plants increased very much in relative importance from 1909 to 1919.[7] At the beginning of this decade less than

7. The figures for 1909 are not as complete as those for later years. But even disregarding this earlier year and comparing 1914 with 1919, the same trend is apparent.

one-sixth of the wage-earners in manufacturing industries were working in plants having more than 1,000 employees; at the end, more than one-quarter were employed in plants of that size. But during the next ten years this trend was reversed, even if the depression year, 1921, is left out of consideration. In 1923, the percentage of employees in the top class was only 24.1 as against 26.7[8] in 1919. In 1929, the culmination of several years of intense activity in many manufacturing industries, of expansion of productive capacity and of corporate growth, this percentage had risen only slightly over 1923, namely to 24.4.

Plant Size in Relation to Size of Industry

If we arbitrarily classify industries which employ a total of 25,000 or more wage-earners as "large" and those which employ less than 25,000 as "small," certain differences between the two classes appear. The most interesting of these is that in the large industries there was a decline—from 28.3 per cent in 1919 to 25.8 per cent in 1929—in the percentage of wage-earners employed in plants having more than 1,000 wage-earners, while in the small industries there was a slight increase—from 16.3 per cent to 17.2 per cent. Just the opposite tendencies appear in the two groups which together embrace plants with more than 250 and up to 1,000 wage-earners. For this category the large industries showed an increase from 27.3 per cent to 29.4 per cent, but the small industries registered a decline from 25.6 per cent to 23.1 per cent.

A breakdown of the total figures by individual industries,

8. Adjusted figure.

the data for which cannot be included in this volume for lack of space, shows that between 1919 and 1929 the number of industries (large and small combined) in which large plants grew in importance and the number of cases in which their importance diminished was even. Conspicuous examples of industries in which the relative importance of large plants increased between 1919 and 1929 are: automobile bodies and parts, from 38.8 per cent to 65.7 per cent of the total number of wage-earners employed; plumbers' supplies, from 11.8 per cent to 28.3 per cent; tobacco (cigars and cigarettes), from 15.4 per cent to 31.6 per cent. Important instances of decreases are: shipbuilding (including boat), from 85.5 per cent to 32.1 per cent; wholesale meat packing, from 64.2 per cent to 43.0 per cent; food preparations, from 9.2 per cent to zero.

The important changes that took place in industrial organization during the twenties were not changes in the size of plants (in terms of the number of wage-earners) but in the size of enterprises. When the size of plants is measured in these terms the concentration movement of the pre-War and War days was suspended. One possible explanation of this is that the size of a plant depends largely upon the technological processes involved. There seems to be an upper limit to size beyond which efficiency decreases under any technological process yet devised. It must be borne in mind, however, that the conclusions in this section are based exclusively on the number of wage-earners, which, as has been pointed out, is only one measure of the size of a plant. Technological developments during the period covered by Table 7 make it entirely possible that if value added by manufacture had been used as a unit of measurement, instead of number of wage-earners, a further increase in the relative importance of large plants might have been evident during the ten years following 1919.

Moreover, variations among different industries make it necessary to accept generalizations based on aggregates with great caution. For instance, consider the growing importance of the large plant in the automobile parts and bodies industry between 1919 and 1929 in contrast with the decreasing importance of the large plant in shipbuilding. It is a plausible assumption that economic factors were as much responsible as technological for this divergence in the concentration of wage-earners in the largest plants.

Concentration of Wage-Earners by Enterprises

It is not the size of the plant, however, as much as of the enterprise, the business entity, that expresses the degree of effective concentration; for, as has been shown,[9] many enterprises in the manufacturing field operate more than one plant.

The *Census of Manufactures* for 1933 recognizes 308 separate industries which are relatively homogeneous in respect to their chief products. While statistics about these industries are published only in terms of the plant, or establishment, as a unit, the Census Bureau has made special tabulations for 84[10] industries for the Twentieth Century Fund, in which there are grouped together the establishments which are under the same ownership.[11] It is thus possible to present, but unfortu-

9. See pp. 35–37.
10. Actually the tabulation includes 85 industries, but data were not furnished for one.
11. The figures for each group of establishments owned by one concern do

nately for one year and for a limited area only, certain facts as to the concentration of wage-earners by businesses within these industries. The list of 84 industries embraces 3,534,836 wage-earners, or 58 per cent of the total number in all manufacturing industries, but it must not be considered as a representative cross-section of manufacturing as a whole. It includes 34 of the 46 *Census* industries which in 1933 employed 25,000 or more wage-earners, but only 50 of the 262 industries which employed less than 25,000.[12]

Concentration in Largest Manufacturing Enterprises

Chart 3 shows the industries arranged in descending order of the proportion of wage-earners in the six largest corporations. It shows also the concentration in the three largest.[13]

The chart reveals striking differences in the degree of concentration. At one extreme is the cigarette industry in which 99.4 per cent of all wage-earners were employed in the eight largest concerns and 91.4 per cent in the four largest; at the other, is women's clothing which had only 3.7 per cent in the

not necessarily represent the total size of that concern, but only its size within the particular industry in question. A business entity often functions in several distinctly different industries, as, for example, an automobile manufacturing enterprise which may also operate plants in the glass and paint industries.

12. The list is somewhat skewed in the direction of higher concentration because of the exclusion of certain large industries in which it was known that there was no appreciable degree of concentration or monopoly, and because of the inclusion of certain small industries in which it was believed that some concentration was likely to be found.

13. It is not definitely known that all of the six or three largest concerns covered by the tabulation are corporations, but in all probability they are. There may, however, be one or two exceptions.

In some industries it was necessary to take seven or eight enterprises instead of six, or four instead of three. In six instances, data are entirely lacking for one or the other group.

CHART 3

Concentration of Wage-earners in Eighty-four Manufacturing Industries, 1933

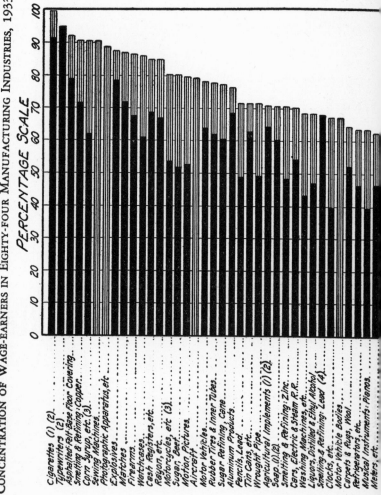

PERCENTAGE SCALE

Cigarettes (1) (2)
Typewriters (2)
Asphalted-Felt-Base Floor Covering
Smelting & Refining; Copper
Corn Syrup, etc. (3)
Sewing Machines
Photographic Apparatus, etc
Explosives
Matches
Firearms
Watchcases, etc.
Cash Registers, etc.
Rayon, etc.
Motorcycles, etc (3)
Sugar, Beet
Motion Pictures
Aircraft
Motor Vehicles
Rubber Tires & Inner Tubes
Sugar Refining, Cane
Aluminum Products
Pencils, Lead
Tin Cans, etc.
Wrought Pipe
Agricultural Implements (1) (2)
Soap, (1), (2)
Smelting & Refining; Zinc
Cars, Electric & Steam R.R.
Washing Machines, etc.
Liquors, Distilled & Ethyl Alcohol
Smelting & Refining; Lead (4)
Clocks, etc.
Motor Vehicle Bodies
Carpets & Rugs, Wool
Refrigerators, etc.
Musical Instruments; Pianos
Meters, etc.

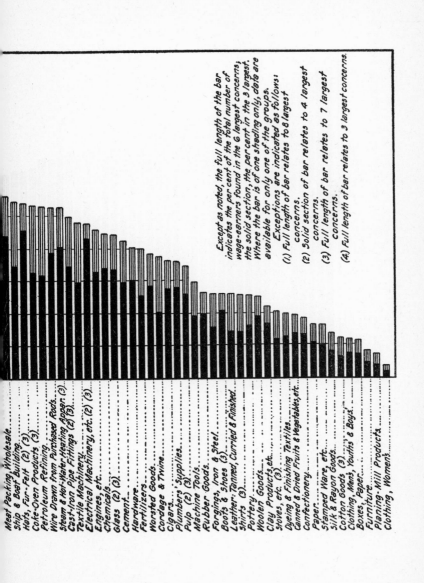

Meat Packing, Wholesale.
Ship & Boat Building.
Hats, Fur-Felt (2) (3).
Coke-Oven Products (3).
Petroleum Refining.
Wire Drawn from Purchased Rods.
Steam & Hot-Water Heating Appar. (3).
Cast-Iron Pipe Fittings (2) (3).
Textile Machinery.
Electrical Machinery, etc. (2) (3).
Engines, etc.
Chemicals.
Glass (2) (3).
Cement.
Hardware.
Fertilizers.
Worsted Goods.
Cordage & Twine.
Cigars.
Plumbers' Supplies.
Pulp (2) (3).
Machine Tools.
Rubber Goods.
Forgings, Iron & Steel.
Boots & Shoes.
Leather: Tanned, Curried & Finished.
Shirts (3).
Pottery.
Woolen Goods.
Clay Products, etc.
Stoves, etc. (3).
Dyeing & Finishing Textiles.
Canned & Dried Fruits & Vegetables, etc.
Confectionery.
Paper.
Stamped Ware, etc.
Silk & Rayon Goods.
Cotton Goods (3).
Clothing, Men's, Youths' & Boys'.
Boxes, Paper.
Furniture.
Planing-Mill Products.
Clothing, Women's.

Except as noted, the full length of the bar
indicates the percent of the total number of
wage-earners found in the 6 largest concerns;
the solid section, the percent in the 3 largest.
Where the bar is of one shading only, data are
available for only one of the groups.
    Exceptions are indicated as follows:
(1) Full length of bar relates to 8 largest
    concerns.
(2) Solid section of bar relates to 4 largest
    concerns.
(3) Full length of bar relates to 7 largest
    concerns.
(4) Full length of bar relates to 3 largest concerns.

six largest and 2.1 per cent in the three largest. The median cases are wholesale meat packing and ship and boat building. In the former, 56.1 per cent of the wage-earners were employed by the six largest concerns and 44.1 per cent by the three largest; in the latter, the corresponding figures are 54.2 per cent and 34.6 per cent.

In 46 of the 82 industries for which there are figures, more than one-half of the wage-earners were concentrated in approximately the 6 largest concerns. In the 80 industries for which there are figures covering the 3 largest concerns, there were 24 in which more than one-half the wage-earners were employed by that number of concerns. There were 31 instances where two-thirds or more of all the wage-earners were in approximately 6 concerns, and 11 where that proportion was found in approximately 3 concerns.[14]

Limitations of Data

Caution must be used in interpreting the chart and these figures. Concentration in the few largest concerns should not be considered apart from the size of the industry and the total number of concerns in it. To illustrate, if an industry had only six concerns it would be meaningless to point out that there was 100 per cent concentration in the six largest. Thus it is not as significant as it might seem at first glance that in the cigarette industry more than 99 per cent of the wage-earners were in 8 concerns. The industry had only 19 concerns in all. Furthermore, a concentration of 70.8 per cent in 6 out of a total of 145 concerns in the agricultural implement industry with

14. See second par. of footnote 13 on p. 42.

11,140 wage-earners, means less than a concentration of 67.2 per cent in 6 corporations in the motor-vehicle bodies and parts industry which had 632 concerns and 145,745 wage-earners.[15]

Average Number of Wage-Earners

An impressive picture of the position of the largest corporations in each industry is obtained by comparing the average number of their wage-earners with the average number in the rest of the industry. Thus in motor-vehicle bodies and parts, the average number of employees per concern was about 230. But the approximate average number employed by the 6 largest concerns was 16,314, while in the remaining 626 it was 76 —a ratio of more than 213 to 1 in favor of the giants. Other high ratios are 201 to 1 in wholesale meat packing (6 concerns against 943); 133 to 1 in electrical machinery, etc. (7 concerns against 1,033); and 95 to 1 in cigarettes (8 concerns against 11).

At the other extreme there are industries in which the average number of wage-earners employed by the small group of the largest concerns is only a few times that of the rest of the industry. Examples of low ratios are 4 to 1 in sugar refining (6 concerns against 7); 5 to 1 in zinc smelting and refining (6 concerns against 13); 5.5 to 1 in matches (6 concerns against 5); 6 to 1 in motorcycles, etc. (7 concerns against 10) and in cast-iron fittings (7 concerns against 43). It appears

15. Industries as classified in the *Census* are in many instances really groups of related industries. For this reason it is possible for a *Census* industry as a whole to show little concentration even though some of its subdivisions might show a high degree.

that in industries where there are relatively few concerns there is likely to be a more even distribution of wage-earners than in those where there are relatively many. The cigarette industry is a notable exception.

Taking the group of 82 industries as a whole, the 512 largest concerns[16] out of the total of 32,445, or 1.6 per cent, employed 37.5 per cent of the wage-earners. The average number of wage-earners for this small number of concerns was about 2,579. On the other hand, 31,933 concerns employed, on the average, approximately 69 wage-earners apiece. The ratio of the large to the small concerns is about 37 to 1. In 80 industries the 249 largest concerns,[17] out of the total of 31,663, or 0.8 per cent, employed 27.0 per cent of the wage-earners in these industries. The average number of wage-earners was 3,647. The remaining 31,414 concerns employed an average of about 78 wage-earners each. The ratio here is more than 48 to 1.

Average Number of Establishments per Concern

In all but four of the industries the average number of establishments per concern was larger for the few largest concerns than for the rest of the industry.[18] This, of course, is to be expected. However, the distribution of establishments per concern was not nearly as asymmetrical as the distribution of wage-earners per establishment. This is also according to ex-

---

16. I.e., the 6 or 8 largest in each industry.

17. I.e., the 3 or 4 largest in each industry.

18. The exceptions are clocks, musical instruments, pianos and watchcases where the average number of establishments per concern was the same for the few largest as for the rest.

pectation. For example, in the motor-vehicle bodies and parts industry the 6 largest concerns employed, on the average, about 213 times as many wage-earners as the average for the remaining concerns in that industry; but they operated on the average only about 6 times as many establishments. The corresponding ratios in wholesale meat packing are 201 to 1 against about 18 to 1.

In general, in those industries in which the difference between the largest concerns and the rest was greatest in respect to average number of wage-earners, the difference was greatest also in respect to the average number of establishments per concern. The size of the industry, in terms either of total number of wage-earners or of total number of establishments, did not determine the distribution of establishments per concern within that industry. Presumably, technological, market or labor considerations did.

Distribution of Value of Products

The distribution of the value of products followed closely the distribution of the number of wage-earners. When there was a high degree of concentration of one of these factors, there was a high degree of concentration of the other. There was a like correspondence when there was little concentration.

Of the 81 industries for which data are available, the percentage of the total value of products produced by the approximately 6 largest concerns was greater than the percentage of the total number of wage-earners employed by them in 40 and was less in 41.[19] Corresponding figures for the ap-

19. In 11 of these 81 industries, however, the difference was so small as to be negligible.

proximately 3 largest concerns in 79 industries show that the percentage of value of products was greater than the percentage of wage-earners in 34 industries, less in 44 and the same in 1.[20]

B. TRADE

Concentration in Wholesale Trade

In preceding pages[21] data were given which showed the extent of concentration in manufacturing in terms of the prevalence of plural units. Corresponding information is available for wholesale trade. As in manufacturing, single unit enterprises predominated in 1929[22] in respect to number, though their supremacy was not nearly as marked—64 per cent of the total as against 88. Table 8 shows the number of enterprises grouped by the number of units controlled, and also the percentage distribution by number of enterprises, by net sales and by total expenses.

While 64.2 per cent of all wholesale enterprises were of the single unit type, only 52 per cent of net sales and 49.8 per cent of total expenses were accounted for by this group. In terms of net sales, the most important plural unit group was that consisting of 6 to 25 units which did 17.6 per cent of the total wholesale business, though comprising only 8.6 per cent of the number of concerns.

20. There were negligible differences in 5 industries.
21. See pp. 35–37.
22. Later data are not available in this form.

TABLE 8

DISTRIBUTION OF ESTABLISHMENTS IN WHOLESALE TRADE,
BY NUMBER OF MARKETING UNITS, 1929[a]

	Total Number of Establishments by Units	Percentage Distribution by Units		
		Number of Establish-ments	Net Sales	Total Expenses
Single units	108,866	64.2	52.0	49.8
2 units	6,225	3.7	5.8	6.1
3 to 5 units	9,191	5.4	9.0	9.7
6 to 25 units	14,584	8.6	17.6	16.0
26 to 100 units	8,304	4.9	7.8	8.3
Over 100 units	19,582	11.5	7.0	9.4
More than 1 unit, but exact number unknown	2,950	1.7	0.8	0.7
Total	169,702	100.0	100.0	100.0

a. Percentages computed from data in *Fifteenth Census of the United States: 1930, Distribution,* II, *Wholesale Distribution,* pp. 92, 94.

Chain Stores in Retail Trade

The degree of concentration in retail trade is revealed through the statistics on chain stores shown in Table 9.

For all fifteen kinds of business combined, chains accounted for one-fifth of the total sales in 1929 and for one-fourth in 1933. They gained in ten businesses, fell back in four and just held their own in one. They made the largest advances in the department store, combination grocery and meat store, the cigar store and the drug store fields.

However it was among the variety stores that chains had their strongest hold. More than 91 per cent of that business was in their hands in 1933. Next in order came shoe stores, where chains accounted for more than 46 per cent of total

TABLE 9

PERCENTAGE OF TOTAL SALES BY CHAIN STORES IN FIFTEEN KINDS OF BUSINESS, 1929 AND 1933[a]

Kinds of Business	Percentage of Total Sales by Chains		Kinds of Business	Percentage of Total Sales by Chains	
	1929	1933		1929	1933
Department stores	16.7	23.9	Grocery stores (no meat)	45.7	45.0
Variety stores	89.2	91.2	Combinations (groceries-meats)	32.2	43.7
Men's stores	21.2	22.0	Restaurants, etc.	13.6	14.9
Family clothing stores	27.3	20.3	Cigar stores—stands	25.1	33.9
Women's apparel stores	22.7	23.4	Filling stations	33.8	35.5
Shoe stores	41.7	46.2	Drug stores	18.5	25.1
Furniture stores	14.2	14.2	Jewelry stores	6.4	5.9
Radio stores	19.1	15.6	All stores	20.0	25.2

a. *Census of American Business: 1933, Retail Distribution,* I, 26–27.

sales. In the jewelry store field, chains were insignificant, with less than 6 per cent of total sales to their credit. Among furniture stores and restaurants they were also of comparatively slight importance.

C. Number of Business Concerns

The figures already presented, fragmentary as they are, tend to show that a process of concentration has taken place in American business. And yet, in spite of this, the number of business concerns has not been decreasing in recent years—except during the depression.

The only official figures on the total number of businesses are those of the Bureau of Internal Revenue which show the number of corporations submitting tax returns since 1909; the number of partnerships since 1917; and, since 1918, the number of individuals with net income, some of which was derived from businesses of which they were sole proprietors. In the next table the first two of these series are given, together with unofficial figures from Dun & Bradstreet.

The number of business corporations reporting to the Bureau of Internal Revenue practically doubled between 1909 and 1930. In the meantime the population of the United States increased only 36 per cent. It is obvious that whatever concentration has taken place in the world of business is not manifested by a decrease in the number of separate enterprises. It is interesting to note, however, that the number of reporting partnerships decreased about one-third from their peak in 1924 to 1933, while the number of reporting corporations decreased only about 3 per cent from their peak which

TABLE 10

NUMBER OF BUSINESSES IN THE UNITED STATES, 1909–1933[a]

Year	Corporations Reporting to Bureau of Internal Revenue[b]	Partnerships Reporting to Bureau of Internal Revenue	Total Listed Concerns, Dun & Bradstreet
	(In Thousands)		
1909	262	...	1,486
1910	270	...	1,515
1911	288	...	1,525
1912	305	...	1,564
1913	317	...	1,617
1914	329	...	1,655
1915	336	...	1,675
1916	341	...	1,708
1917	351	32	1,733
1918	318	104[c]	1,708
1919	320	181[c]	1,711
1920	346	246[c]	1,821
1921	356	265[c]	1,927
1922	383	288	1,983
1923	399	305	1,996
1924	417	321	2,047
1925	430	309	2,113
1926	455	295	2,158
1927	475	283	2,172
1928	496	272	2,199
1929	509	264	2,213
1930	519	245	2,183
1931	516	230	2,125
1932	509	217	2,077
1933	504	215	1,961

a. Bureau of Internal Revenue figures are from *Statistics of Income* for each year since 1918; Dun & Bradstreet figures, from *Vital Statistics of Industry and Commerce,* a special statistical table compiled by that agency.

b. A consolidated return, though representing two or more separate entities, is counted as only one corporation.

c. Including personal service corporations, 1918–1921. If these corporations are excluded, the figures are 101, 176, 241 and 259, respectively.

came in 1930. This is further evidence of the trend toward the corporate form of ownership.

The number of individually owned businesses reported by the Bureau varies so much, because of changes in the law and in the manner in which reports were compiled, that it would be misleading to represent the figures in tabular form. This much, however, they do show: from 1918 to 1923 the number of non-agricultural businesses wholly owned by individuals making income-tax returns rose from 586,043 to 1,560,-698; and from 1925 to 1929 the number of non-agricultural businesses wholly owned by individuals with net incomes of $5,000 or more rose from 189,575 to 209,169.[23]

The Dun & Bradstreet figures, covering corporations, partnerships and individual enterprises, show a nearly 50 per cent increase in the number of "total listed concerns"[24] from 1909 to the peak in 1929. Some part of this increase was probably due to the fact of better coverage at the end than at the beginning of the period. The effects of the depression are seen in the continuous decline from 1930 through 1933.[25]

23. *Statistics of Income*, 1918, p. 11; 1923, p. 9; 1926, pp. 9–10; 1929, p. 13.

24. Dun & Bradstreet defines total listed concerns as ". . . the total of industrial and commercial names in the July issue of the Dun & Bradstreet Reference Book. In general, it excludes financial institutions including banks, railroads, professional enterprises such as lawyers and doctors, farmers and others not ordinarily users of commercial credit in the accepted sense. In general, branches are listed, except in the case of chain distributors."

25. The 1934 and 1935 figures, not given in Table 10, indicate a resumption of the upward trend in the number of businesses. The 1934 figure is 1,974,000, and the 1935 is 1,983,000.

Chapter 4

CONCENTRATION OF CORPORATE WEALTH[1]

PROBABLY THE clearest conception of the position and importance of the large corporation in the American economy can be obtained in terms of wealth (assets) and of income. What proportion of business assets of the nation do the large corporations own; what part of the business income do they earn?

These are complex questions which, for many reasons, elude precise solutions. But though precision is not possible, estimates can be made which are sufficiently reliable to give an essentially correct impression of the situation—statistically. It must always be borne in mind, however, that statistics can be misinterpreted or "over-interpreted."

It must not be assumed, for instance, that the prevalence of large corporations in an industry indicates the extent of control, if any, which these corporations are able to exert over prices, wages, output or trade practices in the industry. Moreover, size has a different significance in different industries. In the public utility and transportation fields, which are to a considerable extent under public regulation, it has a very different meaning from what it has in manufacturing, where problems of competition and monopoly are of pressing importance.

1. See footnote on p. 6.

53

Public utilities are monopolies by nature, and the creation of larger railroad units has been the deliberate aim of Federal legislation.[2] Again, size has a different meaning in industries where basic patents are of fundamental importance; in industries where in order to operate at all a corporation must be large; or under circumstances where the monopolization of raw materials is the concomitant of largeness. These are some of the precautions that should be observed when considering the data that follow.

Less than 600 Firms Own Over Half of Corporate Wealth

Statistics of Income for 1933 reveals a striking concentration of corporate wealth in the hands of a small number of very large corporations; and, conversely, a very large proportion of the total number of corporations with a minute share of the total wealth. The 594 largest corporations (each reporting total assets of $50 million and over and with an average of $240 million) out of a total of 388,564,[3] or 0.15 per cent, owned 53.2 per cent of the total assets of all active reporting corporations submitting balance sheets.[4] If only non-financial corporations are considered, 375 out of 287,575, or 0.13 per cent, owned 56.2 per cent of total assets.[5]

2. Cf. The Transportation Act of 1920.

3. Corporations not filing income-tax returns, and reporting corporations not submitting balance sheets, are not included. The estimated total assets of all these corporations amounted to less than one-half of 1 per cent of the total assets of all corporations.

4. Throughout the analysis of Statistics of Income, references to "all" corporations, "total" corporations, or the like, should be understood to mean "all active reporting corporations submitting balance sheets," even where this is not specifically stated.

5. Corresponding figures for 1932 are: 617 corporations each with assets of

Manufacturing, transportation and other public utilities, and finance accounted for the bulk of the large corporations. Out of a total of 594 $50-million-and-over corporations, 545 —119, 207 and 219, respectively—were in these fields. Only 49 were in agriculture, mining, construction, trade and service combined. Of the 119 giants in manufacturing, 93 were in 3 industries: 19 in food, 29 in chemicals and 45 in metals.[6]

The Other Side of the Picture

There were 211,586 corporations in 1933 with total assets of less than $50,000 each. They comprised 54.5 per cent of the number, but they owned only 1.4 per cent of the total assets. Nearly 95 per cent of the total number of corporations— 367,901—had total assets of less than $1 million each. But this great bulk of business enterprises owned in the aggregate only 14.1 per cent of the assets of all corporations.[7]

The figures bring out a startling contrast between concentration of wealth at one end of the corporate scale and diffusion of wealth at the other. The full extent of concentration is

$50 million and over, and averaging $241 million, were less than 0.2 per cent of the 392,021 reporting corporations submitting balance sheets. They owned 53.3 per cent of total assets. If only non-financial corporations are considered, 386 out of 287,880, or 0.13 per cent, owned 56.8 per cent of total assets.

6. Corresponding figures for 1932 are: 564 out of 617 largest corporations were in the industries named above—117, 215 and 232, respectively. In manufacturing the three largest groups were food (19), chemicals (30), metals (41).

7. Corresponding figures for 1932 are: 206,477 corporations each with assets of less than $50,000. They accounted for 52.7 per cent of the total number of corporations but owned only 1.4 per cent of the total assets. There were 370,309 corporations with assets of less than $1 million, comprising 94.5 per cent of the total of 392,021 corporations, and owning 14.2 per cent of total assets.

to some degree understated because certain corporations controlled by others are separately reported, owing to the fact that they are less than 95 per cent owned by their parent corporations. On the other hand, it must be noted that concentration of corporate wealth is not the same thing as concentration of individual wealth. With few exceptions, the 594 largest corporations are "publicly owned." Thousands, and in some cases several hundreds of thousands of people are stockholders, while a large proportion of the small corporations are owned by a single individual or a family or by a closely restricted group. Widespread ownership of giant corporations means, however, potential rather than actual democratic control. Except under the most unusual circumstances, stockholders neither participate in the affairs of the corporation nor question the activities of the management.

Wide Variations Among Branches of Economic Activity

Overall figures conceal the extremely wide variations among the various branches of economic activity, and even among closely allied groups within each branch. Under trade, for example, there were 120,064 corporations, but these corporations had combined assets of less than $15.7 billion. Obviously trade comprised an aggregation of relatively small corporate units whose average assets in 1933 were only $130,385. Nearly 99 per cent of them had assets of less than $1 million. Transportation and other public utilities, on the other hand, embraced only about one-seventh as many corporations as trade. This comparatively small number of units, however, controlled assets averaging about thirty times as great in value—$3,899,757.[8] In this branch of industry, the number of corporations with total assets of less than $1 million was less than 2 per cent of the total in that industry.

To put it another way, corporations engaged in trade constituted 30.9 per cent of all corporations, while their assets constituted only 5.8 per cent of total assets. Transportation and other public utility corporations accounted for 25.7 per cent of all total assets of all corporations, though in number they were only 4.6 per cent of the 388,564 reporting corporations.

Giant Corporations in Different Industries

The relative importance of the giant corporation varied greatly from industry to industry. In the construction industry the $50-million corporation hardly figured at all. It was of decidedly minor importance in agriculture, in trade and in service—especially in agriculture. But more than one-third of the total assets of the mining industry were in the big business class of that industry in 1933, and not very far from one-half were in that class in manufacturing and finance. The high degree of concentration in finance is of peculiar significance, since the assets of these corporations consist largely of investments in the securities of corporations in other fields. These holdings of financial corporations bring about a further concentration of ownership which extends into all branches of

8. Corresponding figures for 1932 are: 119,346 corporations under trade with aggregate assets of less than $15.8 billion and average assets of $132,041. In transportation and other public utilities there were 17,547 returns showing aggregate total assets of more than $72.1 billion and average assets of $4,111,748.

industry.[9]

In transportation and other public utilities, all but about one-seventh of the assets were held by the giants. It is in this branch of activity that bigness is most conspicuous. But certain divisions of manufacturing also showed very marked concentration of assets. The giant corporations held 55.3 per cent of the assets of the metal industry and 74.5 of the assets of the chemical industry.[10] More minute industrial classification probably would show instances of even more intense concentration in certain specific industries.

Table 11 shows the distribution of corporations among various assets classes and industrial groups. It reveals clearly the different distributional patterns of the different branches of industry; and also the striking lack of correspondence, within each branch, between the distribution of corporations by number and their distribution by assets. Chart 4 shows graphically the relative size of the various branches of industry, as measured by the share of total corporate assets held by each;[11] and, within each branch, the relative importance of the largest and the smallest corporations and of the other size classes combined.

Effect of Investments in Other Corporations

Total assets, though no doubt the most significant measure of corporate wealth, have the disadvantage of including some

9. See pp. 81–92 for a special discussion of concentration in banking.
10. Corresponding figures for 1932 are 54.3 per cent for the metal industry and 74.5 per cent for the chemical industry.
11. Computed after eliminating "Nature of business not given" classification from total.

CHART 4

RELATIVE IMPORTANCE OF VARIOUS BRANCHES OF ECONOMIC ACTIVITY, AND DISTRIBUTION OF CORPORATIONS WITHIN EACH BRANCH, BY VALUE OF TOTAL ASSETS, 1933

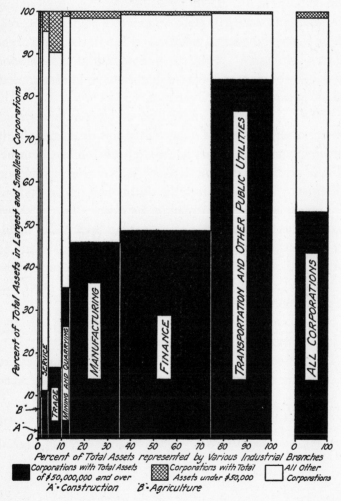

TABLE 11

PERCENTAGE DISTRIBUTION OF CORPORATIONS BY NUMBER OF RETURNS AND BY VALUE OF TOTAL ASSETS, FOR ALL CORPORATIONS AND FOR EACH PRINCIPAL BRANCH OF INDUSTRY, 1933[a]

Total Assets Classes (Thousands of Dollars)	Agriculture		Mining and Quarrying		Manufacturing		Construction		Transportation and Other Public Utilities	
	No.	Assets	No.	Assets	No.	Assets	No.	Assets	No.	Assets
Under 50	44.2	3.7	40.6	0.9	51.2	1.4	69.8	8.6	62.3	0.3
Under 1,000	95.6	45.4	89.5	14.4	93.9	15.2	98.4	49.4	91.6	1.9
1,000 and over	4.4	54.6	10.5	85.6	6.1	84.8	1.6	50.6	8.4	98.1
5,000 and over	0.4	15.2[b]	2.6	67.0	1.5	71.0	0.2	29.0	4.1	95.5
10,000 and over	0.1	8.2[b]	1.2	56.6	0.8	63.9	0.1	22.3	2.7	93.1
50,000 and over	c	9.7[d]	0.2	35.2[b]	0.1	45.8	c	2.7[b]	1.2	83.9

a. Percentages have been computed from data in *Statistics of Income for 1933*, pp. 32 and 172–189. Note that in this and subsequent tables the sum of the figures enclosed by double lines, either vertical or horizontal, equals 100 per cent of the item in question.

b. Estimated. Assets figures not obtainable because of grouping of classes by Bureau of Internal Revenue in order to conceal identity of corporations. The method used in estimating, results in an understatement of assets in the class in which the estimate occurs.

c. Less than one-tenth of 1 per cent.

d. Assets not published by the Bureau in order to conceal identity of corporations, but in this instance the name of the corporation was known, and the assets were taken from its own annual report.

TABLE 11 (continued)

Total Assets Classes (Thousands of Dollars)	Trade		Service		Finance		Nature of Business not Given		All Corporations	
	No.	Assets	No.	Assets	No.	Assets	No.	Assets	No.	Assets
Under 50	68.6	9.5	65.0	4.6	35.1	0.7	65.9	6.6	54.5	1.4
Under 1,000	98.6	48.1	96.5	35.1	90.4	13.8	97.4	57.3	94.7	14.1
1,000 and over	1.4	51.9	3.5	64.9	9.6	86.2	2.6	42.7	5.3	85.9
5,000 and over	0.2	35.1	0.5	37.9	2.1	71.4	0.1	5.3b	1.2	73.7
10,000 and over	0.1	28.5	0.2	28.8	1.0	64.3	0.0	0.0	0.6	67.6
50,000 and over	c	16.6	c	11.2b	0.2	48.6	0.0	0.0	0.2	53.2

b. Estimated. Assets figures not obtainable because of grouping of classes by Bureau of Internal Revenue in order to conceal identity of corporations. The method used in estimating, results in an understatement of assets in the class in which the estimate occurs.

c. Less than one-tenth of 1 per cent.

duplication. A certain proportion, and in the case of financial corporations a very large proportion, of total assets consists of investments in the securities of other corporations.

"Investments other than tax-exempt" is the item in *Statistics of Income* which is the nearest approximation to investments in other corporations that can be obtained from the official statistics.[12] If for 1933 this item ($70,474 million) is deducted from the aggregate of total assets of all corporations ($268,206 million), the remainder ($197,733 million) represents total corporate assets less investments other than tax-exempt. Roughly, then, investments in other corporations amounted to about one-quarter of total assets.

The deduction of this huge volume of investments in other corporations[13] naturally changes materially the absolute magnitude of each of the assets-size classes. That, however, is a matter of little significance. It is of more significance that the relative importance of the various assets classes, especially of the largest, is altered when duplication is eliminated by deducting investments in other corporations, as Table 12 shows.

The relative importance of the smaller corporations increases, and the relative importance of the larger corporations decreases, as the result of deducting investments in other corporations from total assets. This, of course, is because the smaller corporations have trifling investments in other corporations, while the larger corporations have large ones. The 594 corporations in the $50-million-and-over assets class had

12. The item includes an unascertainable, but undoubtedly a relatively small, amount of assets other than stocks and bonds of other corporations.
13. See footnote 12.

approximately 31 per cent of their total assets in investments other than tax-exempt. At the other extreme were 211,586 corporations with only about 4 per cent of their total assets thus invested. Of the more than $70-billion-other-than-tax-exempt investments held by the total of 388,564 corporations, more than 62 per cent was owned by the 594 giants. Approximately 15 per cent more was accounted for by 1,885 corporations in the $10-million-to-$50-million group. These figures suggest that in appraising the position of the largest corporations on the basis of their control of corporate wealth, weight should be given not only to the value of total assets but also to their composition.

TABLE 12

COMPARISON OF PERCENTAGE DISTRIBUTION OF TOTAL ASSETS AND
PERCENTAGE DISTRIBUTION OF TOTAL ASSETS LESS INVEST-
MENTS OTHER THAN TAX-EXEMPT, BY TOTAL
ASSETS CLASSES, 1933[a]

(Total Assets Classes in Thousands of Dollars)

	Percentage Distribution by Total Assets Classes						
	All Classes	Under 50	Under 1,000	1,000 and Over	5,000 and Over	10,000 and Over	50,000 and Over
Total assets	100.0	1.4	14.1	85.9	73.7	67.6	53.2
Total assets less investments other than tax-exempt	100.0	1.9	17.1	82.9	69.9	63.9	49.9

a. Percentages computed from figures appearing in *Statistics of Income for 1933*, pp. 166–167.

Table 13 shows the relative importance of investments other than tax-exempt for each of the major economic groups as a whole.

TABLE 13

PERCENTAGE OF TOTAL ASSETS REPRESENTED BY INVESTMENTS OTHER THAN TAX-EXEMPT, BY BRANCHES OF ECONOMIC ACTIVITY, 1933[a]

Finance	43.4
Nature of business not given	32.9
Construction	20.1
Manufacturing	16.4
Transportation and other public utilities	16.1
Mining and quarrying	11.9
Trade	10.9
Agriculture	9.6
Service	9.3
All branches	26.3

a. Percentages computed from figures appearing in *Statistics of Income for 1933*, pp. 160–165.

Investments in other corporations bulk largest by far in the financial group. Their elimination from total assets would, therefore, affect the relative position of large corporations in this branch of economic activity greatly. It would also be important in "nature of business not given" and in construction. A more detailed breakdown of the 1932 figures (made for this study by the Bureau of Internal Revenue) shows that it is in agriculture, service and finance that the elimination of investments in other corporations has the greatest effect in reducing the relative importance of the giant corporations.

Distribution of Capital Assets

Capital assets consist of lands, buildings and equipment. Control over these assets means immediate control over the physical plant of the country. For this reason their distribution among corporations of various total assets sizes is interesting and significant. The next table shows this distribution, alongside of the distribution of total assets and of total assets less investments in other corporations, i.e., other than tax-exempt.[14]

TABLE 14

COMPARISON OF PERCENTAGE DISTRIBUTION OF TOTAL ASSETS, PERCENTAGE DISTRIBUTION OF TOTAL ASSETS OTHER THAN TAX-EXEMPT, AND PERCENTAGE DISTRIBUTION OF CAPITAL ASSETS, BY TOTAL ASSETS CLASSES, 1933[a]

(Total Assets Classes in Thousands of Dollars)

	Percentage Distribution by Total Assets Classes						
	All Classes	Under 50	Under 1,000	1,000 and Over	5,000 and Over	10,000 and Over	50,000 and Over
Total assets	100.0	1.4	14.1	85.9	73.7	67.6	53.2
Total assets less investments other than tax-exempt	100.0	1.9	17.1	82.9	69.9	63.9	49.9
Capital assets[b]	100.0	1.4	15.0	85.0	73.7	68.1	55.0

a. Percentages computed from figures appearing in *Statistics of Income for 1933*, pp. 166–167.

b. Lands, buildings and equipment, less depreciation.

The distribution of capital assets among total assets classes corresponds very closely to the distribution of total assets.

14. See Table 12, p. 63.

TABLE 15

PERCENTAGE DISTRIBUTION OF CAPITAL ASSETS, BY TOTAL ASSETS CLASSES, IN MAJOR INDUSTRIAL BRANCHES, 1933[a]

(Dollar Value of Capital Assets and Total Assets Classes in Thousands of Dollars)

	Dollar Value of Capital Assets	Percentage Distribution of Total Assets Classes						
		All Classes	Under 50	Under 1,000	1,000 and Over	5,000 and Over	10,000 and Over	50,000 and Over
Agriculture	1,216,556	100.0	3.9	45.5	54.5	c	c	c
Mining and quarrying	6,053,327	100.0	0.9	14.0	86.0	67.8	56.3	c
Manufacturing	24,384,299	100.0	1.2	14.5	85.5	71.8	64.3	45.7
Construction	554,697	100.0	8.7	49.9	50.1	29.5	22.4	c
Transportation and other public utilities	50,140,973	100.0	0.2	1.8	98.2	95.5	92.9	83.1
Trade	3,809,598	100.0	8.7	45.7	54.3	38.5	32.3	16.2
Service	5,069,814	100.0	3.6	34.7	65.3	35.5	25.0	c
Finance	13,712,165	100.0	2.9	44.8	55.2	29.9	21.4	11.1
Nature of business not given	16,925	100.0	8.9	c	c	c	c	c
All branches[b]	104,958,353	100.0	1.4	15.0	85.0	73.7	68.1	55.1

a. Percentages computed from figures appearing in *Statistics of Income for 1933*, pp. 172–189.
b. *Ibid.*, pp. 166–167.
c. Data not available because of grouping of classes.

Not until the highest total assets class is reached is there any noticeable deviation. The giants control a slightly larger percentage of capital assets than they do of total assets. Of all the corporate-owned lands, buildings and equipment, 55 per cent was owned by 594 corporations in 1933 while 387,970 other corporations divided the remaining 45 per cent.

The distribution of capital assets varies greatly among the different industries as can be seen from Table 15.

Only 15 per cent of the physical plant of the country that was owned by corporations in 1933 was owned by those having total assets of less than $1 million. But in construction, agriculture, trade and finance this class owned between 40 and 50 per cent of the capital assets, while, at the other extreme, it owned less than two-tenths of 1 per cent of the capital assets of transportation and other public utilities. In this last-named industrial branch, the $50-million-and-over corporations owned 83 per cent of all capital assets, while in finance the giant corporations owned only 11 per cent. The financial giants, it will be remembered, owned nearly 49 per cent of the total corporate assets in their class.

Chapter 5

CONCENTRATION OF CORPORATE INCOME

A. BY INCOME CLASSES

ANOTHER WAY of measuring the size of corporations is to use income as a yardstick. Figures will now be given to show the distribution of income among various income-size classes. It should be noted, however, that the giant corporations according to assets ($50 million and over) and the giant corporations according to income ($5 million and over) are not two identical groups. The following table classifies corporations reporting net income by three selected income classes over a period of five years.[1, 2]

In 1933 the combined income of almost three-fourths of all corporations equalled less than 3 per cent of the total net income reported. But 69 corporations, or 0.06 per cent of the total number, had an aggregate income in excess of 30 per cent of the income of all corporations reporting net income. Each of the 69 companies comprising this group had a net in-

1. Corporations reporting no net income excluded.
2. All conclusions in this chapter as to changes between years must be looked upon as merely tentative for the reason that the various income and assets classes do not represent identical corporations from year to year. The classes differ each year as to the number of corporations in them, as to the specific corporations which comprise them, and as to the distribution of industrial groups within them.

come greater than $5 million. But the income of each of the great bulk of corporations (74.2 per cent) was below the $5,000 mark. Moreover, by far the larger number of corporations in the $5,000-and-under group reported net incomes of less than $1,000.[3]

TABLE 16

PERCENTAGE DISTRIBUTION OF NUMBER OF RETURNS AND OF TOTAL NET INCOME, BY NET INCOME CLASSES, 1929–1933[a]

Year		Net Income Classes		
		Less than $1,000	Less than $5,000	$5,000,000 and Over[b]
1929	Per cent of total no. of returns	25.8	66.7	0.1
	Per cent of total net income	0.3	2.6	41.9
1930	Per cent of total no. of returns	32.2	74.6	c
	Per cent of total net income	0.5	4.0	39.5
1931	Per cent of total no. of returns	39.9	80.4	c
	Per cent of total net income	0.8	5.2	38.4
1932	Per cent of total no. of returns	50.9	77.5	c
	Per cent of total net income	0.6	3.0	36.4
1933	Per cent of total no. of returns	47.6	74.2	c
	Per cent of total net income	0.6	2.9	30.3

a. *Statistics of Income,* 1929, p. 23; 1930, p. 25; 1931, p. 24; 1932, p. 25; 1933, p. 25. Percentages in the middle column have been computed. The data underlying this table cover all returns showing net income, whether or not accompanied by balance sheets.

b. The actual number of returns in the class having $5 million or more income was: 1929, 300; 1930, 160; 1931, 88; 1932, 59; 1933, 69.

c. Less than one-tenth of 1 per cent.

In 1929, a prosperous year, 300 concerns, or 0.11 per cent of all corporations reporting net income, had incomes of more

3. *Statistics of Income for 1933,* p. 25.

than $5 million, and the combined income of this small fraction of companies equalled almost 42 per cent of the total income of all income-reporting corporations. The income of two-thirds of all companies in that year fell into the less-than-$5,000 class, and the aggregate income of this class was less than 3 per cent of the total net income of corporations reporting net income. The income of almost two-fifths of the concerns in this large group failed to reach the $1,000 level, and their combined income came to only 0.25 per cent of the total of all corporations reporting net income.[4]

B. By Total Assets Classes

From 1920 through 1930 corporations were classified by the Bureau of Internal Revenue only in accordance with the size of their net income. Since 1931, however, there are figures which show the distribution of income among total assets classes. Table 17 presents these for all corporations which reported "statutory net income."[5]

By far the greater number of corporations reported net deficits rather than net incomes during the three years under consideration. But the interest here is in the concentration of the income that was earned by the profitable corporations. In all three years these show a very unequal distribution of statutory net income, as Table 17 demonstrates. The smallest total assets class embraced about 46 per cent of all corporations covered, but accounted for only 2 to 3 per cent of all the in-

4. *Ibid.*, 1929, p. 23.
5. Statutory net income is the compiled net profit less dividends from domestic corporations and interest on tax-exempt obligations. The compiled net profit equals total compiled receipts, less total statutory deductions.

come. Approximately four-fifths of the statutory net income went to those 6 to 7 per cent of the corporations whose total assets were $1 million and over. Only about one-fifth of the income went to the remaining 93 to 94 per cent. The highest total assets class embraced only about one-fifth to one-fourth of 1 per cent of the number of corporations, but this very small

TABLE 17

PERCENTAGE DISTRIBUTION OF NUMBER OF RETURNS AND OF STATUTORY NET INCOME FOR ALL CORPORATIONS REPORTING NET INCOME, BY TOTAL ASSETS CLASSES, 1931–1933[a]

(Total Assets Classes in Thousands of Dollars)

Year		Total Assets Classes					
		Under 50	Under 1,000	1,000 and Over	5,000 and Over	10,000 and Over	50,000 and Over[b]
1931	Per cent of total no. of returns	45.8	94.0	6.0	1.4	0.8	0.2
	Per cent of total stat. net income	3.0	20.1	79.9	66.9	60.1	43.8
1932	Per cent of total no. of returns	45.7	93.0	7.0	1.9	1.0	0.3
	Per cent of total stat. net income	2.0	17.5	82.5	69.7	62.4	45.7
1933	Per cent of total no. of returns	47.0	93.8	6.2	1.6	0.8	0.2
	Per cent of total stat. net income	2.2	20.9	79.1	62.9	55.0	36.0

a. Computed from data in *Statistics of Income*, 1931, 1932 and 1933, p. 32 in each case.

b. The actual number of returns in the $50-million-and-over total assets class which reported statutory net income was: 1931, 265; 1932, 201; 1933, 200.

TABLE 18

PERCENTAGE DISTRIBUTION OF NUMBER OF RETURNS AND OF STATUTORY NET INCOME FOR CORPORATIONS IN VARIOUS INDUSTRIES REPORTING NET INCOME, BY TOTAL ASSETS CLASSES, 1931–1933[a]

(Total Assets Classes in Thousands of Dollars)

Year	Manufacturing		Transportation and Other Public Utilities		Trade		Finance	
	Under 50	50,000 and Over	Under 50	50,000 and Over	Under 50	50,000 and Over	Under 50	50,000 and Over
1931 Per cent of total no. of returns	41.6	0.2	54.6	1.2	58.9	b	31.1	0.2
Per cent of stat. net income	1.4	42.7	0.1	72.1	8.0	33.6	3.7	26.4
1932 Per cent of total no. of returns	37.8	0.3	50.1	1.5	59.8	b	34.3	0.2
Per cent of stat. net income	1.1	40.7	0.6	70.5	5.3	30.9	3.2	29.8
1933 Per cent of total no. of returns	34.6	0.2	52.3	1.3	57.1	0.4	36.8	0.2
Per cent of stat. net income	0.9	30.8	0.8	68.4	5.8	25.4	3.6	17.6

a. Computed from *Statistics of Income*, 1931, pp. 161, 173, 175; 1932, pp. 167, 179, 181; 1933, pp. 173, 185–186, 188.

b. Less than one-tenth of 1 per cent.

fraction of the total accounted for between 36 and 46 per cent of the income in that class. Note, however, that in 1933 the relative position of the largest corporations was less impressive than it had been one and two years earlier.

Variations Among Industries

The distribution of income among total assets classes varies widely from industry to industry. The following table shows the distribution for the largest and the smallest assets classes for the four industries for which there are figures.

Several interesting facts are brought out in Table 18. The percentage of statutory net income of the largest total assets class in each group ranged, in 1933, from 17.6 per cent, for financial corporations, to 68.4 per cent for transportation and other public utilities. Similar spreads appear in the two other years covered. There is relatively, though of course not absolutely, an even wider range in the smallest assets class.

In each of the four industries a marked decline in the percentage of total statutory net income earned by the largest total assets class took place between 1931 and 1933. The year 1932 was between 1931 and 1933, except in the case of financial corporations. The percentage of statutory net income of the smallest total assets class was less in 1932 than in 1931 in each of the four industries, but it was slightly larger in 1933 than in 1932 in three of the four industrial groups.

Compiled Net Profit Less Income Tax

The item in the *Statistics of Income* tabulation most closely comparable to net income as ordinarily reported to stockholders is the compiled net profit less income tax.[6] In 1931, the 265 largest income-reporting corporations, according to assets, accounted for 49.8 per cent of this total item, although they constituted only 0.18 per cent of the total number of firms. In 1932, the 201 largest, or 0.27 per cent of all corporations reporting net income, had 50.3 per cent of the total compiled net profit less income tax, and in 1933 the corresponding figures (covering 200 corporations) were 0.2 and 40.6 per cent, respectively.[7] Incidentally, it is worth noting that the only class in all three of these years which showed a plus value for total compiled net profit less income tax, considering all returns together, was the small group of large corporations with assets of $50 million and over.

C. CONCENTRATION OF ASSETS AND INCOME COMPARED

Table 19 compares the concentration of total assets, statutory net income and compiled net profit less income tax for corporations having total assets of $50 million and over.

For the group of giant corporations covered by Table 19, there was a much greater degree of concentration of assets than of income, whether expressed as statutory net income, or as compiled net profit less income tax. The proportion of income earned by the largest corporations fluctuated more than the proportion of assets owned by them. Although the larger corporations just about held their own in assets during the

6. The compiled net profit equals the total compiled receipts less the total statutory deductions. Income tax includes a small amount of excess profits tax in 1933.

7. Percentages computed from *Statistics of Income*, 1931, pp. 32, 156–157; 1932, pp. 32, 162–163; 1933, pp. 32, 168–169.

period, they lost in income. The figures in Table 19, it should be remembered, refer only to corporations reporting net income, and indicate only the relationship of the largest corporations (assets of $50 million and over) to the other corporations in this group.

TABLE 19

COMPARISON OF PERCENTAGE DISTRIBUTION OF ASSETS AND INCOME OF LARGEST CORPORATIONS REPORTING NET INCOME, 1931–1933[a]

Year	No. of Corporations with Total Assets of $50,000,000 and Over, Showing Net Income	Percentage of Total for All Income-Reporting Corporations Accounted for by $50,000,000-and-Over Total Assets Class		
		Total Assets	Statutory Net Income	Compiled Net Profit Less Income Tax
1931	265	56.0	43.6	49.8
1932	201	61.6	45.7	50.3
1933	200	55.8	36.0	40.0

a. Percentages computed from *ibid.*, 1931, 1932, 1933, p. 32 in each case.

Comparisons for Separate Industries

Table 20 compares concentration of assets and concentration of income[8] in the $50-million-and-over total assets class for four separate industries.

This table shows how misleading generalizations can be. While it is true that, when all industries are considered in the aggregate, "a much greater degree of concentration of assets

8. Income distribution confined to statutory net income. Data on compiled net profit less income tax not available for separate industries.

than of income" is shown, this statement is not true of trade by itself. In this field, in each of the years covered, there was a greater concentration of statutory net income than of total assets. Furthermore, the discrepancy was much greater in finance than in either manufacturing or in transportation and other public utilities.

TABLE 20

Comparison of Percentage Distribution of Total Assets and of Statutory Net Income of Largest Corporations Reporting Net Income, by Industries, 1931–1933[a]

| | Percentage of Total for Each Classification Accounted for by $50,000,000-and-Over Total Assets Class | | | | | | | |
| | Manufacturing | | Transportation and Other Public Utilities | | Trade | | Finance | |
Year	Per Cent Assets	Per Cent Income	Per Cent Assets	Per Cent Income	Per Cent Assets	Per Cent Income	Per Cent Assets	Per Cent Income
1931	47.9	42.7	81.8	72.1	23.4	33.6	51.7	26.4
1932	51.4	40.7	79.6	70.5	25.9	30.9	61.7	29.8
1933	49.5	30.8	79.1	68.4	23.2	25.4	54.5	17.6

a. Percentages computed from *Statistics of Income*, 1931, pp. 161, 173, 175; 1932, pp. 167, 179, 181; 1933, pp. 173, 185–186, 188.

D. Consolidated vs. Unconsolidated Firms

The annual issues of *Statistics of Income* throw some light on the position of corporations filing consolidated reports.[9]

9. ". . . a consolidated return may be filed when one or more chains of corporations are connected through stock ownership with a common parent corporation, at least 95 percent of the stock of each of the corporations (except the

Not all such corporations are large; nor do all large corporations file consolidated reports. Figures for gross income, however, do indicate that consolidated reports are found primarily among the corporations in the larger assets-size classes, as is to be expected. In 1933, for example, the average gross income of corporations making consolidated returns was more than 37 times as large as the average gross income of all non-consolidated corporations.

Of the 617 largest corporations in 1932, 361, or about 58 per cent, made consolidated reports.[10] Since, however, there were 7,426 consolidated returns filed in that year, it is evident that slightly more than 95 per cent of all consolidated reports represented relatively small corporations. In number of subsidiaries, consolidated reports covered a great size range— from 1 to 282 in 1932. The average was four. Information as to what percentage of the 594 largest corporations in 1933 filed consolidated returns is not available. It probably did not differ appreciably from 1932.

Income Reported by Consolidations

In 1929, 8,754 consolidated returns were filed, which represented 1.7 per cent of all corporation returns. Of these, 5,408 showed a net income, and this number was 2.0 per cent of all

common parent) being owned directly by one or more of the other corporations, and the common parent corporation owning directly at least 95 percent of the stock of at least one of the other corporations." *Statistics of Income for 1933*, p. 32.

10. Letter of September 23, 1935 from the Treasury Department to the Twentieth Century Fund, Inc., gives these figures and points out that there were 617 corporation returns for 1932 with total assets of $50 million and over, instead of 618, as published in *Statistics of Income*.

corporations reporting a net income. But the 2.0 per cent in number accounted for about 51 per cent of the aggregate net income of all net income-reporting corporations.[11] The non-consolidated corporation returns—98 per cent of all those reporting net income in 1929—accounted for 49 per cent of the aggregate net income.

TABLE 21

PERCENTAGE DISTRIBUTION OF NET INCOME BY INCOME CLASSES,
1933: CONSOLIDATED RETURNS REPORTING NET INCOME
COMPARED WITH NON-CONSOLIDATED RETURNS
REPORTING NET INCOME[a]

| | Net Income Classes | | | | | |
| | Less than $1,000 | | Less than $5,000 | | $5,000,000 and Over | |
Type of Return	Per Cent of Total Returns	Per Cent of Total Income	Per Cent of Total Returns	Per Cent of Total Income	Per Cent of Total Returns	Per Cent of Total Income
Consolidated	8.9	b	24.0	0.1	1.4	51.9
Non-consolidated	48.3	0.8	75.1	4.0	b	21.9

a. Percentages for consolidated returns computed from figures appearing in *ibid.*, pp. 34, 48. Percentages for all returns other than consolidations computed from figures derived by subtracting figures for consolidated returns from figures for all returns.

b. Less than one-tenth of 1 per cent.

This was the situation in the boom year, 1929. In the depression year, 1933, it was different. Then there were only 7,101 consolidated returns and these represented only 1.4 per cent of

11. *Statistics of Income,* 1929, pp. 26–27. In some instances the percentages have been computed from basic data.

all corporation returns[12] as against 1.7 per cent in 1929. There were 1,880 consolidations reporting net income and this was only 1.7 per cent of all corporations reporting net income—a slight drop from the 2 per cent of three years earlier. But the share of total net income which went to the consolidated group showed a drastic decline, namely from 51 to 27.9 per cent of the net income of all corporations reporting net income.

The distribution of income by income classes differs widely between corporations filing consolidated returns and all other corporations. The comparison is made for three classes in Table 21. The point to note is that the consolidated reports show a very much greater degree of concentration of income in the largest income-size class.

Variations Among Industrial Branches

The area of incorporated business represented by consolidated returns varies greatly among the different branches of industry. As usual, it is misleading to talk about aggregates without indicating these variations. Table 22 brings out the differences among the principal economic branches. Gross income is used as a basis of comparison in order to permit the inclusion of all reporting corporations—those showing deficits as well as those with net incomes.

These figures reveal the inequalities in the importance of consolidated returns in the different principal branches of economic activity. In manufacturing, not far from one-half of the gross income went to corporations making consolidated

12. *Ibid.*, 1933, p. 33.

returns; in mining and quarrying, nearly 60 per cent; in transportation and other public utilities, nearly 70. But in construction less than one-seventh of the gross income was consolidated income; in finance only slightly more than one-sixth; in trade less than one-fifth.

TABLE 22

Comparison of Gross Income of All Corporations and Gross Income Represented by Consolidated Returns, by Industrial Branches, 1933[a]

Industrial Branch	Gross Income of All Corporations[b]	Gross Income Represented by Consolidated Returns	Per Cent of Total Gross Income Represented by Consolidated Returns
	(In Thousands of Dollars)		
Agriculture	395,130	126,521	32.0
Mining and quarrying	1,958,275	1,160,841	59.3
Manufacturing	35,150,775	16,281,472	46.3
Construction	1,078,549	147,866	13.7
Transportation and other public utilities	10,609,249	7,315,153	69.0
Trade	24,198,944	4,630,272	19.1
Service	2,821,208	752,182	26.7
Finance	7,420,748	1,275,513	17.2
Nature of business not given	9,542	27	0.3
Total	83,642,421	31,689,844	37.9

a. *Statistics of Income for 1933,* pp. 23, 24, 33, 34.
b. Whether or not submitting balance sheets.

Chapter 6

CONCENTRATION IN BANKING

CONCENTRATION IN banking is of peculiar significance because the banking system exercises an important influence on industry and business as a whole.

In the development of commercial banking, the years since 1900 may be divided into two periods. These show sharply divergent tendencies. Until about the end of 1920 the trend was toward a diffusion of facilities and of resources. The number of banks increased, not only absolutely but also in relation to the growth of population. Measured by their capital stock outstanding the average size of banks declined. In terms of resources, the average per bank fell slightly between 1900 and 1914, but rose sharply between the latter year and 1920.[1] A somewhat similar trend is evident when size is measured in terms of total capital funds per bank.

Since 1921, however, there has been a considerable decrease in the number of independent banks. On the other hand, the number of branch offices operated has shown a large increase, and there has been a rapid growth in group and chain banking. The decline in active banks is mainly due to the large number which, since the latter part of 1920, has been forced

1. Neither trend, however, was regular.

to suspend operations and go into liquidation. To a lesser degree it is accounted for by the elimination of banks through merger or consolidation, either voluntary or involuntary, that is to ward off actual failure.

Because of the large proportion of small banks among those which have gone out of business since 1921 as a result of developments referred to above, an increasing part of the country's banking resources has become concentrated in the larger institutions.

The Period of Diffusion[2]

Between 1900 and 1920, the number of banks of all types increased from 10,382 to 30,139—or by about 190 per cent. If private and savings banks are excluded, there was an increase of about 229 per cent—from 8,391 to 27,633. Over the same period, population increased by only 38.9 per cent.

The trend toward smaller institutions, especially between 1900 and 1915, is indicated by the decrease in average capital stock per bank from $167,000 to $141,000 for national banks, from $54,000 to $35,000 for state commercial banks and from $435,000 to $287,000 for loan and trust companies. Notwithstanding a reversal of this downward trend after 1914, the 1920 averages were still only $152,000, $51,000 and $338,000, respectively.

Total capital funds (capital stock, surplus and undivided profits) of the three groups of banks averaged, respectively,

2. The figures in this section are from the *Annual Report of the Comptroller of the Currency* for various years. All figures from this source are as of, or about, June 30.

$271,000, $84,000 and $949,000 in 1900; $266,000, $56,000 and $634,000 in 1915; and $342,000, $92,000 and $773,000 in 1920. On this basis, therefore, only loan and trust companies were smaller in 1920 than in 1900.

Average resources per bank in 1915 were moderately higher than in 1900 in the case of national and private banks, and strikingly higher in the case of mutual savings banks. Between 1914 and 1920 the average increased markedly for each type of bank. The figures for the latter year were well above those for 1900. For all banks, average resources were $1,039,000 in 1900 and $1,761,000 in 1920.

A more complete picture of this movement toward diffusion is obtained by noting that, in 1899, 32.9 per cent of all commercial banks had less than $50,000 capital stock each, as against 59.0 per cent in 1920. In 1899 these banks with less than $50,000 capital were all state banks, and constituted 61.6 per cent of all active state banks in that year. By 1920 this proportion had increased to 69.2 per cent. National banks of this size increased from none in 1900 to 32.5 per cent in 1920.

The Period of Concentration: Bank Failures

Among the several factors which, until more recently, have caused the concentration of banking resources in the larger institutions, by far the most important is the elimination from the banking system of large numbers of small institutions through failure.

From 1921 through 1932, 10,816 banks were closed on account of financial difficulties. Of these closed or "suspended" banks, 1,614 had been permitted to reopen prior to January

1933, so that for the twelve-year period the number of permanently closed, or failed, banks was 9,202.[3] These failures represented about 30 per cent of all active banks reported on June 30, 1921, and almost 35 per cent of the average number of active banks during the period. Deposits involved in these failures amounted to more than $4 billion. This sum was about 10 per cent of the deposits of all active banks at the beginning of the period, and approximately 8 per cent of the average deposits.[4]

Of the total number of banks suspended during 1921–1932 by far the greater proportion were relatively small institutions. Those with capital stock of less than $25,000 constituted over 34 per cent of the total number and those with less than $100,000, over 85 per cent.[5] On the other hand, suspensions of banks with capital stock of $1 million and over amounted to only slightly more than one-half of 1 per cent of the total number.[6] The preponderance of small banks is shown further by the fact that more than 91 per cent of all suspended banks had less than $1 million of loans and investments each. But these accounted for about 42 per cent of the total of loans and investments involved in bank suspensions.[7]

3. Computations based on figures appearing in *Twenty-first Annual Report of the Federal Reserve Board, 1934*, p. 167, Table 80.

4. This total of $4 billion does not include an unknown amount of deposits in 102 private banks. Cf. *Twentieth Annual Report of the Federal Reserve Board, 1933*, p. 221, note 2.

5. Percentages have been computed not on the basis of the total number of bank suspensions noted above (10,816), but on the number of banks for which the capital stock was known, namely 10,693.

6. *Twenty-first Annual Report of the Federal Reserve Board, loc. cit.*

7. *Report of Federal Reserve Committee on Branch, Group and Chain Banking*, "Bank Suspensions in the United States, 1892–1931," p. 41.

Events subsequent to the banking holiday account for a substantial portion of the decrease in active banks since 1921. Between January 1, 1933 and March 16, 1933, 449 banks, with deposits of more than $215 million, were suspended. During the remainder of that year, 179 licensed banks,[8] with deposits of more than $145 million, were suspended, and during 1934, 57 banks, with deposits of almost $37 million. Furthermore, of the 4,194 banks with deposits of nearly $4 billion which were not licensed as of April 12, 1933, 2,113 banks with deposits of $2,524 million had been placed in receivership up to December 31, 1935. Including 34 banks with deposits of $10 million suspended during 1935, the total number of banks permanently closed on account of failure during the period 1921–1935 was, therefore, 12,034, with deposits of $7,024 million.[9, 10]

Bank Consolidations

A second important cause both of the decrease in the number of active banks since 1921, and of the concentration of the country's banking resources in larger units, has been the increased tempo of the combination movement. The consolidation or merger of two or more banks was by no means a rare phenomenon even prior to 1921. Probably not less than 2,300

8. I.e., banks that had been permitted to resume operations, without restrictions, after the conclusion of the bank holiday on March 16.

9. *Twentieth Annual Report of the Federal Reserve Board, 1933*, p. 206; *Twenty-second Annual Report of the Board of Governors of the Federal Reserve System, 1935*, p. 176.

10. In this total no consideration has been given to the number of licensed banks suspended during 1933, 1934 and 1935 which subsequently were permitted to reopen, no figures being available.

mergers, involving about 4,500 banks, took place between 1900 and 1921.[11] These mergers increased the size of a good many banks. Their effect upon the banking system as a whole, however, was more than offset by the large increase in the number of newly chartered banks of small size.

During the next eleven years, 1921–1931 inclusive, there were 5,094 bank mergers involving 9,538 banks.[12] As a result, 5,137 institutions ceased to exist. But instead of an increase in the number of new small banks to offset this tendency toward concentration—as during the first two decades of the century —8,036 banks were permanently closed subsequent to failure and only about 3,000 new ones were established. This net decline of more than 5,000, plus the decrease of 5,094 banks through merger and consolidation, accounts for about 10,100 of the decrease of approximately 10,500 banks between early 1921 and the end of 1931.[13]

Branch Banking[14]

As a corollary to the concentration movement, a rapid increase occurred in the proportion of the country's banking resources controlled by banks operating branches. Until recently, this has been due more to the extension of city-wide than of state-wide branch banking.

11. Cf. John M. Chapman, *Concentration of Banking*, pp. 53–60.
12. *Ibid.*, p. 56.
13. This estimate does not take into consideration the decrease caused by voluntary liquidations, for which no data are available.
14. Sources for this section are: Unpublished data compiled by the Federal Reserve Board; *Federal Reserve Bulletin*, April 1930; *Twenty-second Annual Report of the Board of Governors of the Federal Reserve System, 1935; Annual Report of the Federal Deposit Insurance Corporation for the Year Ending December 31, 1935.*

Between 1920 and 1930 the number of commercial banks operating branches increased from 530 to 770; and the number of branches operated, from 1,280 to 3,334. At the end of 1933, however, only 575 banks operated branches, totaling 2,752.

As a result of the large decrease in the number of active banks, and notwithstanding this recent decline in branches, the proportion of banking facilities represented by branches has steadily increased. Moreover, recent years have witnessed a recovery in the number of branches, partly the result of the extension since 1933 of branch banking in several states which had until that year prohibited such activities. Thus, at the end of 1934, the number of commercial branches was 3,017, while on December 31, 1935, 820 commercial banks in the Continental United States operated 3,149 branches.

The extent of the concentration movement is shown by the fact that branches represented 4.2 per cent of the total number of commercial banking facilities (banks and branches) in 1920, 13.2 per cent in 1931, 15.5 per cent in 1933, 16.4 per cent in 1934, and 17.1 per cent at the end of 1935.

The true character of the branch-banking movement is better seen when expressed in terms of resources or deposits. In 1920, resources of banks operating branches amounted to $9,592 million, or about 18 per cent of the aggregate of all banks; in 1929 they amounted to $33,269 million, or 46 per cent. Although a decline to 41 per cent was recorded for the year 1931, it would appear that recent years have witnessed an upward trend. Thus, on December 31, 1935, commercial banks operating branches controlled deposits amounting to

$22,759 million, representing 51.5 per cent of the total of $44,265 million of commercial banking deposits in the Continental United States.

Branch banking has developed mainly in seven states, and excepting California, mainly in the form of head office-city branch banking. The extension of branch banking in several states after the 1933 banking holiday, together with the elimination of independent banking facilities in other regions of the country, has, however, given some impetus to the establishment of county and outside-county branches. Thus the entire increase in branches during 1935 was accounted for by branches outside head office cities, while city branches decreased.

Leading branch banking states at the end of 1935 were California with 798 branches, New York with 671, Ohio with 169, Massachusetts with 149, Michigan with 147, New Jersey with 118 and Pennsylvania with 107 commercial and mutual savings bank branches.

Group and Chain Banking

Branch banking is, of course, a type of "concentration" because of the centralized control over resources. So, likewise, are group and chain banking. Though differing from each other in many respects, they are very much alike in their effect upon the tendency toward centralization in the banking field.

The number of banks controlled by groups and chains on December 31, 1931 was 1,886. The number of controlling groups was 273. The total loans and investments of these banks amounted to $9,642 million. The largest number of banks controlled by groups and chains was 2,229, reported as of June 30, 1930. The largest number of groups and chains, 332, was reported as of December 31, 1929. But the amount of loans and investments controlled by groups and chains was highest on June 30, 1931, namely, $13,355 million.[15]

Increase in Relative Importance of Larger Banks

As has been shown, failures, mergers and the growth of branch banking have resulted in a considerable decline in the number of banks. This, in turn, has meant the concentration of an increased proportion of the country's banking resources in fewer banks. Group and chain banking, while not decreasing the number of banks, have furthered the movement toward the centralization of banking resources by providing unified control over nominally independent institutions.

The increase of recent years in the relative importance of the larger national banks is proved by the figures in the following table.

Table 23 shows that the biggest national banks, measured by capital stock, have gained vastly in relative importance between 1925 and 1934. In number they remained insignificant, but their share of the total assets of all national banks rose from slightly more than one-fourth to not much less than one-half.[16] All other capital stock classes lost ground over the

15. John M. Chapman, *Concentration of Banking,* chapters XIV and XX; also H. Parker Willis and John M. Chapman, *The Banking Situation,* chapter XVI. Cf. also *Report of the Federal Reserve Committee on Branch, Group and Chain Banking* (1932).

16. The distribution of loans and discounts and of total deposits in every year and for every class corresponds very closely to the distribution of total assets.

TABLE 23

NATIONAL BANKS CLASSIFIED ACCORDING TO CAPITAL STOCK: PERCENTAGE DISTRIBUTION BY NUMBER AND BY TOTAL ASSETS, 1925 AND 1929–1934[a]

Per Cent of Total

Capital Stock (Thousands of Dollars)	1925		1929		1930		1931		1932		1933		1934	
	No.	Assets	No.	Assets	No.	Assets	No.	Assets	No.	Assets	No.	Assets	No.	Assets
Under 50	30.2	3.8	27.7	2.9	27.2	2.6	26.5	2.4	26.0	2.1	24.1	1.8	19.7	1.4
50–200	53.0	21.1	53.6	18.2	53.6	16.6	53.9	16.4	54.3	15.3	54.4	13.8	56.5	12.4
200–500	10.9	14.9	12.1	13.1	12.5	12.3	12.8	12.7	12.7	11.8	13.6	11.0	15.0	10.8
500–1,000	3.0	8.9	3.5	8.0	3.6	7.8	3.6	7.7	3.6	7.1	4.1	7.3	4.8	7.9
1,000–5,000	2.6	23.8	2.6	17.9	2.5	16.7	2.6	17.4	2.8	18.0	3.1	19.7	3.3	20.3
5,000 and over	0.3	27.5	0.5	39.9	0.6	44.0	0.6	43.4	0.6	45.7	0.7	46.4	0.7	47.2

a. Percentages computed from data in various issues of the annual reports of the Comptroller of the Currency. All figures are as of December 31 each year, except those for 1925 which are as of June 30.

period, the losses being heaviest in the two smallest classes.

The giant banks made almost all of their inroads on the other classes between 1925 and 1930. Since 1930 their rate of advance has been greatly retarded, and they have shared their gains with the $500,000–$1,000,000 and the $1,000,000–$5,000,000 classes.

The Twenty Largest Banks

More evidence of increasing concentration in banking is the growing proportion of the total loans and investments of all banks held by the country's twenty largest banks. This is brought out in the following table.

TABLE 24

PROPORTION OF TOTAL LOANS AND INVESTMENTS OF ALL BANKS
HELD BY THE TWENTY LARGEST BANKS,
SELECTED YEARS, 1900–1931[a]

Year	Per Cent Held By Twenty Largest Banks	Year	Per Cent Held By Twenty Largest Banks
1900	15.1	1928	18.1
1920	13.8	1929	21.2
1925	15.2	1930	24.8
1926	15.7	1931	27.3
1927	17.1		

a. Reproduced from Willis and Chapman, *op. cit.,* p. 143. Figures computed by the Federal Reserve Committee on Bank, Group and Chain Banking.

Between 1900 and 1920, the twenty largest banks lost some ground, relatively. This, of course, was the result of the great increase in the number of small banks during that period.

With the reversal of this trend after 1920, the largest banks began to recover their lost ground. They have gradually absorbed a continually greater proportion of the banking business. After 1928 the increase was very rapid, primarily the result of the many mergers of already big banking institutions. In 1931, the twenty biggest banks held very nearly twice the proportion of assets they did in 1920.[17]

Corresponding figures have not been published for the years after 1931, but data on deposits indicate that the largest banks continued to improve their relative position. In 1930, the twenty-five biggest institutions held 30 per cent of the deposits of all banks in the United States, exclusive of mutual savings banks. By 1935 their proportion had risen to 38 per cent—a gain of more than one-fourth.[18]

17. It should not be assumed that the 20 banks are the same each year throughout the period.
18. *American Banker,* January 21, 1936, pp. 1, 5.

Chapter 7

CONCENTRATION OF THE TOTAL NATIONAL INCOME PRODUCED

THE RELATIVE importance of corporations of various size groups has now been measured against the background of total corporate wealth and income. More significant, however, of the relative positions of the small, medium and large corporations is the distribution of the total national income—corporate and non-corporate—produced by each of these groups. Table 25 presents the figures which, because of the nature of the underlying data, must, however, be looked upon as nothing more than reasonable estimates. Chart 5 illustrates the relationships in four major groups of economic activity and in industry as a whole.

The position of the largest corporations varies enormously for the different industrial divisions for which there are figures. In transportation and other public utilities, giant corporations predominate, representing about two-thirds of all the business. In manufacturing they represent about one-third; in finance, about one-sixth; in trade, only about 7 per cent. In mining and quarrying, corporations with total assets of $5 million and over account for slightly more than three-fifths of the national income produced by that branch of economic activity.

CHART 5

PERCENTAGE OF TOTAL INCOME PRODUCED BY CORPORATIONS
OF VARIOUS TOTAL ASSETS CLASSES IN FOUR MAJOR
DIVISIONS OF ECONOMIC ACTIVITY AND IN
INDUSTRY AS A WHOLE, 1933

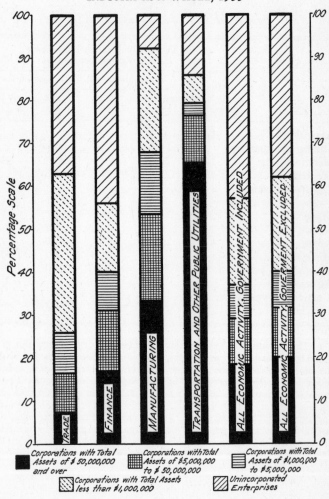

TABLE 25

PERCENTAGE DISTRIBUTION OF THE TOTAL NATIONAL INCOME
PRODUCED BY CORPORATIONS OF VARIOUS TOTAL ASSETS
CLASSES, BY MAJOR DIVISIONS OF ECONOMIC
ACTIVITY, 1933[a]

(Total Assets Classes in Thousands of Dollars)

| | | Per Cent of Total National Income for Each Group Produced By— | | | |
| | Unin-corporated Enterprises | Corporations with Total Assets of— | | | |
		Less Than 1,000	1,000–5,000	5,000–50,000	50,000 and Over
Agriculture	94	3.1	2.9[b]	...	...
Mining and quarrying	4	19.8	15.4	60.8[c]	...
Manufacturing	8	24.3	14.3	20.0	33.4
Construction	67	23.4	5.0	4.6[c]	...
Transportation and other public utilities	14	6.5	2.9	11.1	65.5
Trade	37	37.0	9.5	9.1	7.4
Service	67	19.3	5.0	8.7[c]	...
Finance	44	16.0	9.0	14.0	17.0
Miscellaneous	62	28.2[d]	9.8[e]	...	0.0
All economic activity	43	20.1	7.9	10.6	18.4
All economic activity, government excluded[f]	38	21.8	8.6	11.6	20.0

a. The percentage of the total income in each field of industry that is produced by corporations in the various size classes has been assumed to be about the same as the ratio of the total compiled receipts of corporations in each class to the total compiled receipts of all corporations in the industry. The estimates of the proportion of total income produced in each field that can be attributed to corporations (see p. 17) are based on 1929 figures. However, it appears that 1929 figures present a fairly normal picture of the relative importance of the major branches of industry and of the extent to which income produced is under the control of corporations. Total compiled receipts are from *Statistics of Income for 1933*. The figures in the above table were derived as

In construction and in service the $5-million-and-over corporations[1] are of comparatively slight statistical significance.

Nearly One-Fifth of Income Produced by 594 Corporations

Taking American industry as a whole, both incorporated and unincorporated enterprises, the 594 corporations with assets of $50 million and over—only 0.1 per cent of the total —produced 18.4 per cent of the total national income in 1933. That such a small number of firms should have done not far from one-fifth of the nation's business is remarkable. And yet the great bulk of American economic activity—more than 81 per cent of it—is still in the hands of unincorporated enterprises (including government) and of small and medium-size corporations. If government is omitted as a field of economic activity, the largest corporations are shown to have controlled 20.0 per cent of the profit-seeking business of the country in

follows: The percentage distribution of total compiled receipts for all reporting corporations submitting balance sheets was first computed from data appearing in *Statistics of Income for 1933*, pp. 172–189. These percentages were then "stepped down" to obtain the distribution of total income produced, instead of merely of corporate income. This was done by applying the estimates of incorporation contained in Table 3 of the present volume. Example: The $50-million-and-over corporations in manufacturing accounted for 36.4 per cent of the total compiled receipts of all reporting corporations submitting balance sheets in 1933. Manufacturing is estimated to be 92 per cent incorporated, on the basis of income produced. Therefore the $50-million-and-over corporations in manufacturing produced 36.4 per cent × 92.0 per cent of total national income produced, or 33.4 per cent.

   b. Total assets of $1,000,000 and over.
   c. Total assets of $5,000,000 and over.
   d. Total assets of under $500,000.
   e. Total assets of $500,000 and over.
   f. The reasons for including government among the income-producing activities is stated on p. 16, footnote 4.
   1. I.e., the two right-hand columns combined.

1933;[2] while the unincorporated firms, together with the corporations having total assets of less than $1 million, controlled nearly 60 per cent. The remaining 20 per cent is accounted for by corporations with total assets of more than $1 million but less than $50 million.

2. In 1932, the giant corporations accounted for 19.3 per cent of total national income produced, government included, and 21.0 per cent, government excluded.

16,181

Chapter 8

CONCLUSIONS

FROM THE mass of figures bearing on the place of the large corporation in American economic life some important conclusions can be drawn.

In the first place the picture is not a simple one. It is just as true to say that big business does not predominate in America as to say that it does. It all depends on the angle from which the picture is viewed, or on the focus of attention on details.

If the entire panorama of economic activity is kept in view the large corporation is far less prominent on the scene than if the attention is focussed on the area of incorporated concerns. And if the focus is concentrated on some particular industries big business looms large; while if other specific industries are under examination big business simply does not exist.

Two Viewpoints

The picture can be painted in two sharply contrasting colors. For example, taking the broadest view, it can be truthfully said that 81 per cent of all American economic activity is carried on by the medium or small corporations, by firms which are not incorporated at all or by individuals. More than two-fifths of the entire business activity in the United States is not in corporate hands at all—much less in the grip of the giants. Of the total national income produced, the corporations with $50-million-or-more assets produced only 18.4 per cent in 1933. From this point of view the large corporation sinks into relative insignificance.

By concentrating attention only on that particular 57 per cent of our economic life which is carried on by corporations, it can just as truthfully be said that 594 corporations out of the 504,080[1] that existed in the United States in 1933—or one-tenth of 1 per cent—own more than half the assets of all corporations put together. Or to put it in another way, 95 per cent of all corporations in the United States own only slightly more than 14 per cent of all the corporate assets. This sounds as if American business were completely dominated by big business. And such is a very common opinion.

Yet this is just as "colored" a picture as the other. Both pictures are true at the same time and both must be kept in mind if the realities are to be firmly grasped.

Details Reveal Variations

Coming closer to the scene, it is clear that some groups of industries are far more in the hands of giant corporations than are others. For example, in agriculture only about 6 per cent of the total income produced is produced by corporations, and the share of the one $50 million agricultural corporation[2] is negligible. Again, in construction only one-third of the in-

1. This figure includes inactive corporations, and active corporations not submitting balance sheets.
2. As a matter of fact, only a part of the activities of this corporation are in the field of agriculture, and the corporation would generally not be regarded as agricultural, although it files its tax reports as such.

come produced is produced by corporations, and of those corporations the $50-million-and-over concerns possess but 2.7 per cent of the industry's total corporate assets.

At the opposite extreme are the transportation and other public utilities, the mining and quarrying and the manufacturing industries. Each of them is over 85 per cent incorporated— mining and quarrying, 96 per cent. The biggest corporations in the public utility field are only 1.2 per cent of the total in number but they own 83.9 per cent of the industry's corporate wealth. In mining the giants are but 0.2 per cent in number but they represent 35.2 per cent of the assets; while in manufacturing the giants number 0.1 per cent but control 45.8 per cent of the wealth.

Coming even closer to the scene, a view of the separate manufacturing industries reveals still greater variations. Consider the cigarette industry, which is at one end of the scale, and the women's clothing business which is at the other. The eight largest concerns making cigarettes employed 99.4 per cent of all the employees in the entire industry, while in women's clothing the six largest employed but 3.7 per cent of that industry's total workers.[3] In the cigarette industry big business is predominant; in women's clothing it hardly exists.

Again, focussing attention on those industries in which the large corporation predominates, two facts must be kept in mind. One is that, with comparatively few exceptions, the great business enterprises of the country are owned not by a small number of individuals but by thousands, and in a few

3. It should be remembered that figures on wage-earners are from the Bureau of the Census and not from the Bureau of Internal Revenue.

cases by hundreds of thousands, of stockholders. This is important, even though at present, except under unusual circumstances, a bridgeless chasm exists between the large body of rank-and-file stockholders with potential control and the small group of insiders which actually exercises it.

Turnover Among Giants

The second fact, perhaps of even greater significance, is the "turnover" within the group of industrial giants. There are giants each year, but they are by no means always the same giants. Bankruptcy takes a high toll of even the largest companies. It is, of course, a fact that receivership or bankruptcy often means only legal death. The corporation, especially if it has large capital assets, is likely to be reorganized and continue in business, sometimes even with very little change in management. Nevertheless, bankruptcy means the failure to attain the end for which business concerns are formed—profits; it is proof that size does not give exemption from risk; and since it frequently involves serious loss to investors it acts to some extent as a deterrent from future similar investments.

Of the 101 largest industrial corporations in 1919, twenty either went into receivership, or reorganized with a write-down of capital in order to avoid receivership, at some time before the end of 1934. Of the 106 largest industrial corporations at the beginning of 1930, twelve went into receivership or bankruptcy, and two more reorganized to avoid bankruptcy, before the end of 1934.[4]

4. The figures in this and the remaining paragraphs are based on an analysis of the giant corporations listed by Berle and Means in *The Modern Corporation and Private Property*, pp. 19–24.

Eight of the 46 largest utilities in 1919 went into bankruptcy, or reorganized with loss to stockholders, before the end of 1934; another was saved only by being taken over by the state. Of the 52 largest public utilities in 1930, 7 went into receivership before the end of 1934.

The record of the railroads was even worse. Of the 48 largest railroads in 1919, 14 were in bankruptcy before the end of 1934. Of the 42 largest railroads in 1930, 11 have since gone into bankruptcy.

The mortality rate among the giant corporations in the fifteen-year period from the beginning of 1920 to the end of 1934 was 19.8 per cent for industrials, 17.4 per cent for utilities and 29.2 per cent for railroads.

Whole Story Not Told

One final word must be added. The figures presented in this volume do not tell the whole story of the concentration of wealth and income in the hands of the giant corporations. Concentration can be effected and control exercised in ways that are not subject to statistical measurement—for example, through interlocking directorates, investment trusts, trade associations and banking affiliations. It is beyond the scope of this volume to discuss these and similar instruments of concentration and control, but their existence should be kept in mind when appraising the evidence in the foregoing pages.